EMBRACING
DEATH

Riding Life's
Transitions into
Power and Freedom

Angela Browne-Miller

BEAR & COMPANY
PUBLISHING
SANTA FE, NEW MEXICO

LIBRARY OF CONGRESS CATALOGING-IN-PUBLICATION DATA
Browne-Miller, Angela,
Embracing Death : Riding Life's Transitions into Power and Freedom /
Angela Browne-Miller

ISBN 1-879181-38-X

Bear & Company, Inc.
Box 2860
Santa Fe, NM 87504-2860

Cover Illustration: Robert Pasternak

Cover and interior page design: Melinda Belter

Text illustrations: Leona Jamison

Author Photograph: Swift Silver Photo

Editing: Sonya Moore

Printed in the United States of America by BookCrafters

9 8 7 6 5 4 3 2 1

*this book is dedicated
to the beings who have
guided its transmission
and inspired the dissemination
of its message,
speaking only for the right use of will
in the name of the ever purest
and ever highest
of ever lasting
Light*

CONTENTS

Author's Note

This book offers an introduction to the death technologies. Readers have a right to such knowledge. Readers also have a responsibility to apply such knowledge with care and with the highest ethical intent. May these words and all their applications support only the right use of will and only the clearest elaboration of energy of the highest order.

ONE

INTRODUCTION TO DEATH

Embracing Death is written for anyone who is undergoing, has undergone, or will undergo death or a major ending or transition of any sort. This includes divorce, being fired, leaving home, or having children leave home. It includes abrupt changes or endings such as having a home collapse in an earthquake, receiving a serious injury, or having something precious stolen. It also includes gradual but definite changes such as: changes in behavioral patterns—for instance, shifting out of a steady or an addictive relationship to a drug, a person, a behavior; outgrowing a stage of life, a philosophy, a religion, or a cult; aging; having all of your oldest friends die; or undergoing the disease process, whether it is temporary, chronic, or terminal. And, of course, included is the model of death with which we think we are so familiar:

1

physical death, which is seen by many people as the ultimate of all deaths. Indeed, physical death—fear of it, avoidance of it, viewing it as final—is an excellent model for all the deaths, small and great deaths, that each and every one of us must endure.

The word "endure" is used here because all deaths can be endured: you *can* make it through any ordeal, no matter how impossible "making it through" seems to be, no matter how impossible the transition appears to be. On some level, you already know this. You have already been through many profound transitions in your lifetime. You have been born, you have walked your first steps, you may have been breast-fed and then weaned. You probably had a first day of school, had a favorite pet die, became an adolescent, fell in love for the first time, had sex for the first time, broke up with your first boy- or girlfriend, finished school, left home, got hired, maybe have been laid off or fired, married, divorced, mourned the death of a family member or friend, or have experienced some other life change. Of course, not all of these are considered unpleasant or difficult experiences. Why, then, refer to them in this book about death? All changes, whether they seem to be "good" or "bad," are types of deaths. We must allow ourselves to stretch the meaning of the word "death" this way in order to fully understand death. Death itself, as are most painful experiences, is painful when we cannot see it as otherwise. We must learn how to see what we think of as "painful experiences" as otherwise and to use them well. Look back on your life. Think of the many experiences—the changes, the losses, the graduations, the departures, the crises—you found difficult or painful as they were happening, then later saw as "not so bad," useful, maybe even great!

Death, the death of anything—your marriage, your way of life, your body—is a transition, a passage. It would be dishonest to say that death is not an ending. It is an ending *and* a transition into a new beginning. It is how you navigate this transition that will set the stage for your next beginning. The more you understand the process, the great adventure of death, the more you incorporate into your repertoire the death technologies described here and in subsequent volumes, the more you can use the death experience to consciously, with your full attention at work upon it, create the next phase of your life, design your new reality.

Death in any form is, indeed, a great adventure. It is a challenging, wondrous, remarkable journey every time you take it. No two deaths are the same; however, the passage we call death has characteristics that can be identified again and again. Learning to recognize these characteristics, these landmarks along the road of transition, will ease your passage, will enhance the richness of your experience, will ensure your survival (in the form of survival you learn to choose), and will determine the

quality of the survival—the richness of the harvest—you
take from your death.

And you *can* harvest your death. Even if it is one of
the more difficult passages you may undergo during your
on-Earth life—a divorce or other family breakup; a major
downturn in financial, career, health, or social status; a
physical disaster of some sort; or physical death itself—
you can transform the process. You can transform it from a
miserable ordeal, a disaster through which you seem to be
aimlessly and hopelessly tumbling, into a profound initiation.

Even physical death is a great initiation. On some
level we are aware of this. Yet, few people consciously prepare for this initiation-by-physical-death or any of their
other initiation-by-living-death adventures. This is because we tend to be afraid of great changes, of great risks,
of great unknowns. So we do not consciously plan for
them, except to buy insurance, write wills, and pray for
some kind of salvation or direction. However, it is not
only fear that keeps us from preparing for initiation-
by-death. Fear is one of four mental conditions that keep
us from knowing how to plan for, manage, take control
of, successfully endure, and harvest all our dying processes. Next to fear is our deep programming, the behavioral
and energetic patterning we are programmed to be
addicted to. And next to pattern addiction is lack of
information: We have not been taught the true nature of

death. We have either denied ourselves or have been denied the truth about our existence. And beyond these states of mind is the social state of mind—the cultural taboos and laws we have developed and enacted against learning how to die well, against actually dying a physical death with grace and at will. This is not to advocate suicide as an impulsive, desperate way out of the challenges of life. This is, however, to advocate in favor of an adult individual's right to die—your right to choose for yourself (and for no one but yourself) the time, place, and method of your own death, so long as you are making a responsible choice.

You can decide for yourself how much emotional and physical suffering you choose to undergo in any of your dyings, physical or otherwise. Why do most of us not know this? Consider the possibility that we have been denied the truth about death—by religions, by political leaders, by those among us who know (whether they be on- or off-planet forces). Why deny us truth? We are much easier to control if we spend our energy worrying about, avoiding, or denying death. We are much easier to control through our fears, our pattern addictions, our lack of information, and our religious and legislative taboos.

Were each and every one of us able to transform crisis into opportunity; to ride personal, social, and global disaster; personal, social and global apocalypse; personal, social, and global death into heightened awareness, into greater energy, and into power, we would be an entirely different people. We would be more powerful as individuals and as a collective life force. Whatever forces (from within or outside) hold us, our spirits, captive will be severely threatened when we become masters of our own deaths. Death masters can set their spirits free.

We who seek to inform you are inviting you to become exactly this: a master of death. This will enable you to master your life. After all, we are always living and dying. And so is the world. Rethink the concept of death for yourself and for all humanity. Your survival and freedom, our survival, our freedom, depend upon the spreading of this awareness.

You will grow to understand this on a deep level as you read through this book. These ideas about the death process will flow into your intelligence gently and allow you to take them as lightly or profoundly as you wish, as you feel ready for.

Thank you for joining us in embracing death. This experience, this journey, is yours. So make it your own! Master the ride of your life. Meet death, all kinds of death, and know life on all levels. The time has indeed come for the removal of our ignorance. Death is not to be feared. Death is the greatest adventure.

TWO

THE APOCALYPSE SYNDROME

Now we are ready to unmask death and see its face. The mask itself is surprisingly easy to remove. Yet, behind the mask are many layers of faces. Close to the surface is the crust of our fear, the fear we project onto the death experience.

DISTINGUISHING BETWEEN FEARS

Let's examine this fear. Think of times you have been afraid. Did you ever examine your fear? Was your fear a help or a hindrance to you? This is an important distinction. To master death, whatever the sort of death or transition being faced, we must see the difference between the two basic types of fear, one a help and one a hindrance to survival.

When used well, fear serves a purpose; though, when

used well, what we call "fear" is better described as *pro-tective awareness*. For example, being afraid of an auto accident does less to prevent an accident than does being very alert, highly aware of the other vehicles, people, animals, and the state of the road. Paying attention is a very good idea. Being so scared that you cannot protect yourself is not a good idea. When fear clouds the consciousness, it is not being used well; it is *blinding fear*.

This distinction between protective awareness and blinding fear is also valuable when transferred from the individual to the population or social level. Not everyone who warns us of physical, environmental, political, economic, or other danger or disaster is sick with blinding fear. Some of these persons are calling important developments to our attention, suggesting that, in order to have a *conscious say in* or *conscious response to* the course of events, we pay attention and maybe even take action. Too often, those who seek to alert us to things, events, or forces that may affect us undesirably and against our wills are criticized or labeled "paranoid" or "overly fearful" or "crazy." This is unfortunate, as protective awareness is of great value to all living things, including humans. A respectable futurist or prophet is often taken far too lightly.

The problem is that we have a hard time knowing what to believe, how to tell the difference between useful information coming out of protective awareness and the static and chaos coming from the projection of blinding fear. We humans have lived with so many fear-inducing lies for so long that we confuse these with valid warnings of impending danger. It becomes frighteningly difficult to tell the difference.

DEFINING APOCALYPSE

Why are we unable to clearly sense this difference between protective awareness and blinding fear? We have been genetically, culturally, and spiritually programmed to carry within us a condition, frequently manifesting as a disease, that we can call the *apocalypse syndrome*.

The term "apocalypse" comes from the Greek word "apokalypsis," or "disclosure." Apocalypse is some kind of major all-involving disaster in which forces of good and evil clash, and in which, in the end, only supernatural intervention can preserve good.

Take some time to think about the meaning of apocalypse and what your conscious mind does with this concept. Whether or not your subconscious mind pays any attention to this concept is less important for the moment. Just think about how apocalypse is understood.

According to most definitions of apocalypse, communication with divine forces reveals the timing, the force, and the characteristics of an apocalypse. Many religions therefore include "divine revelation." Some of these revelations are said to come to all humans directly from God;

however, in said reality, apparently only a few humans can read them. Many other revelations come from God but through designated go-betweens or intermediaries who may be witch doctors, shamans, religious leaders, or persons with special abilities or special statuses.

Most major religions include references to one or more apocalypses or cataclysms. These are said to take place at the end of a cycle of time. At the end of such a cycle, piety will be dead; fire, drought, and famine will ravage Earth; then a century or a millennium or a long spell of death will follow. Only some will remain alive: They are "the remnants." Despite flooding, all the moisture on and in Earth will begin to dry up. Eventually, a universal conflagration of some sort will eliminate the last of the human occupants and all physicality of Earth will be consumed in a vast whirlpool of flame. There is usually a "supernatural" way for "the believers" and "the chosen ones" among the very last of the remnants to survive in some other dimension of reality.

This is standard apocalypse. Depictions of this process appear again and again in human religion and mythology. Many of these myths include the same ingredients—increasing tribulation and the moral dissolution of human kind; the emergence of some kind of major war; the fracturing and collapse of Earth's crust, and later, the sinking of land masses, even entire continents, into the sea; the atmosphere becoming darkened; stars (including comets and meteors and maybe even moons) crashing down to Earth from the sky; and a massive fire of some sort filling much of the atmosphere.

Of course, this end is also a beginning, as new *yugas*, time cycles, begin after major apocalypses, with the same cycles appearing repeatedly. Eventually, the same ultimate fate evolves. Again and again, from the spoils, from the ashes of the cosmic fire, arises the phoenix, the flight of life resurrected, born anew.

This quick overview is not to minimize the reality of apocalypse. Modern science tells us that Earth has surely witnessed comet impacts and massive disasters of global proportions that killed off entire groups of species— dinosaurs, for example. And we do not know the extent of it. There is more to history on Earth than we teach ourselves. Much of the truth about Earth's history has been lost. However, collective memory has managed to keep some form of this information alive for us all, pre- serving it not only in mythical and religious form throughout history, but also in symbolic imagery deeply imbedded in that collective memory or mind—perhaps even in the genetic codes that are part of that mind. Here, we must pause to wonder, if images of apocalypse are indeed coded into our collective memories, how did those images get there and are they placed there to protect us or to scare us into being more easily controlled?

Personal Apocalypse

Whatever its means of and motive for coming to us may be, information about the possibility of global or massive disaster is useful. Humankind desires this knowledge. Humanity instinctively keeps its sensors out, maintaining a protective awareness regarding past and potential global cataclysms. The problem is that with this healthy instinct comes a deeply buried blindness. Even if various people do not feel themselves to be fearful, they cannot help but be affected by imagery buried deep within the collective mind. These traditionally and genetically preserved visions bring on the great Fear of Death.

This discussion is important in that it traces the source of our individual awareness of possible disaster back through human history and Earth history to images of actual disaster that have indeed taken place and can indeed happen again. Every living thing has deeply ingrained survival mechanisms that should promote an ongoing protective awareness in each of us. But we somehow translate this high and pure awareness down into a lower emotional state that clouds the intelligently protective consciousness. The great Fear of Death thus becomes dangerous baggage carried on our precious journeys through, and in and out of, our lives on Earth.

Many people bring awareness and acceptance of the reality of global, solar, galactic, even cosmic, cataclysm down to the personal level. As a result of this instinctive translation, they start seeing potential apocalypse everywhere. Protective awareness and blinding fear are then mingled. Perceptions are then clouded and very subjective. This is how personal apocalypses, real or imagined, are tailor-made for us, by our subjective perceptions of our experiences and of the information we have regarding possible upcoming experiences. These personalized apocalypses include and confuse real and imagined, global and local, population and personal, minor and major traumatic life experiences.

And, to further cloud the issue, as problematic as this confusion is, it contains within it some degree of honesty: A child screaming in pain on the other side of the planet is felt by a sensitive person standing here. This sort of sensitivity is group or population awareness. On some level, all of us are always in touch with the sensations being experienced by members of our own species, wherever they are, and even by other life forms everywhere. Some breast-feeding mothers have discovered this sensitivity when their babies cause them to drip milk by screaming, even out of earshot, somewhere across town! We are all this sensitive, whether we recognize it or not. This is a basic survival mechanism—sensitivity to the needs of the species. Personal apocalypse consciousness is a reality, whether a person is conscious of having it or not. Population pain *is* personal suffering—even when this translation is entirely subconscious.

POSITIVE APOCALYPSE CONSCIOUSNESS

Apocalypse awareness is with us. It would be dishonest to say that intense experiences, challenging transitions, events that may be perceived as terrible, will never take place. But it would also be dishonest to say that there is no positive way of seeing these.

Positive apocalypse consciousness is knowing how to detect for yourself the difference between blinding fear and protective awareness, and how to resist labeling sensations as one or the other of these fears when others label them for you. Positive apocalypse consciousness also involves a sense of rising to meet the challenge of any transition, of any death. Seeing a purpose, a positive outcome, as a distinct possibility—even if that positive outcome is simply that you *can* make it through an ordeal—is indispensable. Positive apocalypse consciousness is essential. This constructive view and use of our instinctive apocalypse awareness will purify the application of protective awareness and reduce its being mingled with blinding fear. *Embracing Death* herewith covers the basics of this positive consciousness.

Allow the ideas offered here to dialogue with your heart, mind, and soul. Move in between the following words and lines and sense their meaning. Question as much of this as you feel driven to. Honest questioning and ongoing dialogue are a means of discovering truth for yourself. And this is the surest route to knowledge.

THREE

PHYSICAL DEATH AS A MODEL

No discussion of death can go on without some review of the phases of physical death (as experienced by human life forms on Earth). This is not only because physical death is what is most commonly thought of when the word "death" is said. It is also because physical death is a fantastic metaphor for many other endings, crises, and transitions. You will see the value of this comparison between physical and other forms of death as you read on. Try not to allow a fear of death or the sense that "this has nothing to do with my life right now" to stop you from really reading this chapter. All your transitions, especially the more difficult ones, are quite similar to physical death. All deaths have detectable stages or phases. All deaths challenge the dying to stay conscious through the process.

THE PROCESS OF PHYSICAL DYING

Each and every physical death is different; however, there are general similarities among them all. Some of the variation in the dying process relates to the style of death chosen (if we have or take the opportunity to choose, that is).

It is important to know how to stay connected to your consciousness while you die. Conscious dying is your right *and* your responsibility. Conscious dying can take place whether or not a person is medically defined as being "conscious." Quite often, but not always, the first end-phase of physical dying is experienced semiconsciously. Where it is not, the dying person is nevertheless more conscious and aware than he or she may appear. Usually, as the dying process intensifies, blood pressure substantially drops. The brain therefore finds itself running short of its normal supply of oxygen and sugar. So it turns on a compensatory mechanism that dilates its blood vessels and draws extra blood from wherever it might be stored in the body. This gives the sugar-hungry brain a brief increase in blood sugar. The brain hangs on to its biologically fueled inner consciousness this way.

At this point, the brain is, for a brief time, receiving a much enriched supply of food. With this increase in brain food the dying person is able to flash back or even to rapidly review his or her entire life. Consciousness is actually intensified then, although little emotion is felt in these flashback moments. This is because this high speed memory review is a higher cognitive activity, with little if any involvement of lower emotional processes.

The brain, mainly the cortex, is working at a feverous pitch. It is consuming sugar faster than it can get it. This results in the brain's sensing that it cannot continue to fuel the intense flashback process. When this awareness is registered, the brain begins moving into the second end-phase of physical dying. It is operating at a very high frequency then, maintaining what are called rapid rhythmical beta waves with some spurts of alpha. This generates what some human meditators can bring about for themselves without dying—a sense of bliss, a sense of transcendence.

Whether or not it appears to be conscious in medical terms, the brain is quite conscious of this state of euphoria or intense happiness. Yet this is not really an emotional experience in the way we experience joy in daily life. This is a very special, very high, state of emotional bliss.

This phase of physical dying draws to a close. Up to this time, medical or other efforts to revive the dying person, to return the dying person to the mortal body, can still be successful. However, many a dying individual, persuaded by the profound euphoria, is committed to dying by now. Now the dying person wants to die this death.

Remember, and you will indeed remember these

words, that when you find yourself in this state, you do have a right to move on. At this point in your own dying, it will be important to understand that you can still easily make a conscious decision to either go ahead and die or to come back into your body. You can actually make this decision without medical intervention pushing you in either direction. You are actually quite powerful at this juncture. You just need to know you are to be so.

If the dying person moves on into death, the third end-phase of physical dying begins here. Now the body will stop breathing. The physical eyes will stop seeing, although they have most likely stopped looking before this time. The brain will stop functioning, being out of sugar, and will choke on its waste matter. The dying individual is quite aware of these sensations in a detached way.

Some dying individuals still manage a return to their physical bodies at this late phase of dying. Should you feel a tug to return to your body when you find yourself in this phase of death, examine the tug to determine who or what is pulling on you. Note your response to this tug. Be conscious of your choice at this time. Make certain it is indeed *your* choice. Do not linger in indecision. Let the body die as soon as possible if you are leaving it. Do not unwittingly leave your "empty" but still living physical body open to inhabitation by an essence other than your own.

Focus on, even enjoy, this third end-phase of death. The last words, if any, will have been uttered—usually mumbled or whispered—by now. One of the last physical sensations is the feeling, again not unpleasant, that the mouth is filled with something as thick as but not as unappealing or as physical as cement. This is actually the cement of the ether, the nonphysical reality into which the dying person is now moving. There will be no further physical sensation unless the dying individual imagines there to be. This is tricky because the imagination cannot arise from the brain at this point. Most persons who are able to be conscious during this time will feel that they are not in their bodies. Remember that this is a good time to observe how much of your sensation of reality you can conduct with what you think of as your mind, whether or not you have a functioning body, working sensory organs, or a living physical brain.

Now there is a continued awareness of self, and a looking at the body that is being shed. Some beings now see people touching or kissing their corpses and experience detached longings for their physical bodies again. Others are relieved to let go. Stay conscious here. Notice when your "mind" is seeing, feeling, "thinking." Notice your location in what you have been calling space and time. Pay close attention to this wondrous transition.

FREEING THE SOUL

Letting go is critical here. You should remember that you can stay conscious as you do so. It is important to understand the letting go or severance process. Physical death is a great teacher of severance. Only true severance allows us to really move on.

Physical death severance is the withdrawal of the soul from its two anchors: the heart and the pineal gland in the brain. This withdrawal from the heart and from the head cuts off the two streams of energy, the blood stream and the endocrine stream or system, that unite the ethereal soul with the physical body. This cutting off severs the connection between body and soul. Sometimes a body resists the departure of the soul that has inhabited it and then this severance process is slow and messy. It might be better said that some souls, not understanding this process, do not fully cut these cords, these streams between the dimensions. If you stay quite conscious here, *you* can be the one to cut these cords, these umbilical cords, for yourself, and deliver yourself into a new dimension of reality. You can be the creator and keeper of the new cord of your death transition. Just integrate these details of the death transition into your conscious awareness. Try to envision yourself going through these changes.

So, now you are finished with the end-phases of physical death. Once you pass out of the body or physical vehicle, you have passed from the first episode of death or the first death, which is physical, to the second death, which is not physical. In this next death comes what is called the "astral death"—the death of the emotional vehicle. And you have grown quite a large emotional body during this lifetime!

Once the physical house of the body is empty, it begins to decompose. You may want to think that death is complete at the physical end, after the phases of physical death described above. Yet, the next dying, that astral death, is as much a great passage, if not more. The individual who has just lost her or his body still retains many of the feelings and awarenesses of others' feelings acquired while in that body.

A highly trained being, practiced in the death technologies, can leave the physical vehicle quite consciously and, in full waking awareness, fully preserve the continuity of consciousness while moving from the physical plane to the after-death state. You can do this relatively well, whether or not you have received intensive training, if you can stay conscious and remember that all your emotions are part of an emotional body that you are shedding. Even love, in its material plane manifestation, must be shed. See this shedding as a purification. This purification is an opportunity to make room for the purest, most serene sensation, a far higher, nonemotional love, to come to you. This pure sensation, this "high love," does not attach

itself to emotional (astral) or physical bodies. If you stay
stuck to low level love and other emotions, you remain
trapped in your emotional body; your consciousness,
energy, and power weaken. Those who do not understand
this second stage of death—emotional death—enter it
hysterical, fearful, angry, and/or bewildered and needless-
ly waste their spiritual energy.

Try to take this information in by studying it from
time to time. You will remember bits of this description
many times during your livings and dyings. You may also
want to read more intricate reviews of the dying process
and the details of its stages than we have space for here.

Eventually, whatever her or his awareness, the physically dead individual must die the second death, must
leave behind all emotional connection to the physical
plane and move on. This letting go is a critical and very
difficult process for many a soul. At this point, the soul
senses that what comes next is the dissipation of all the
mental energy—which still lingers *after* the emotional
energy has been shed—assumed during the recent incarnation. This is the third death.

It is said that very few spirits are "evolved enough" to
succeed in fully completing this third death and, in so
doing, crossing the threshold beyond the "death cycle." It
is also said that most fail at this death and therefore must
recycle again and again until some day they will finally
succeed. We ask you to be alert here and question this

particular message. The message is not wrong; however, the surrendering of mental energy must be studied closely. When you die this third and final phase, where does your mental energy go? Where do you go? Do you want to go there? Are you willing to stay conscious right on through all the very challenging phases of the death process in order to look closely at where you are sending your precious human energy at this juncture?

NAVIGATING DEATH

You must consciously navigate your death in order to avoid surrendering your mental energy—energy *you* cultivated, most likely during your physical lifetime—to a force that may use it for other than what you would freely choose to have it used. Accept responsibility for this awareness. If you can, you will be able to free countless souls from being cycled against their wills through the human energy plantation and other farms and factories such as this one throughout the Cosmos. We will return to this profound matter later. (See Chapter 11.)

Whatever conscious focus is achieved by the dying individual on moving through even the first two, the physical (or actual) and the emotional (or astral) episodes of death, will serve as great training for that soul. The intelligent, survival-oriented, road map from physical to astral *to mental death* is one drawn by repeated exploration of the process. Navigating the three deaths well is the greatest challenge for a being.

And here is the metaphor: navigating the death process. There is an art and a science *and a politic* of dying that we can learn and apply to all types of transitions.

A QUESTION OF RIGHTS

Your right to die in the manner you choose for yourself must be exercised while you are on Earth and in your physical body as well as in the period after you leave your body. Human rights extend far beyond the physical plane. We need you to take them there. You need to practice taking them here, on Earth, now.

FOUR

ALLOWING OUR PATTERNING TO DIE

We often describe ourselves and each other as "creatures of habit." Think about what this means—we are robots—nice, soft cuddly ones maybe, but nevertheless, programmable machines. Should we allow ourselves to be such? Is this what we choose of our own free will?

This chapter is included to explain that a healthy death—even a death within a life, the death of a behavior —can free the spirit trapped within the robot, can eliminate undesirable programming *and can protect against ongoing brainwashing.* The following discussion of pattern addiction, which some of us actually call automatic brainwashing, is essential to your recognition of true freedom, and to your understanding of your life and all your dyings, large and small.

OUR RIGID ADDICTIONS TO LIFE AS WE KNOW IT

There is more to our resistance to death than either blinding fear (of the known or unknown) or protective awareness. There is also a deep, genetically ordained drive within every genetically coded living organism to become addicted to patterns. And this is, for the most part, a survival-oriented tendency. After all, it is essential that we respond automatically and rapidly, without taking the time to think, to life-threatening situations. It is also convenient that certain necessary behaviors become habitual. How many people would stop their cars at red lights on time if they had to use seconds to figure out what the red lights signified?

It is good that we do some things automatically. But there is a down-side to this automatic programming capability of ours. We have begun to recognize the downside. In recent times, humans have become increasingly conscious of the problem of addiction to destructive and dangerous patterns such as compulsive overeating, drug addiction, alcohol addiction, sex addiction, relationship addiction, domestic violence and other compulsively violent behaviors, and workaholism. These are *explicit* addictions —the more obvious, visible addictions. These behaviors tend to be more easily recognized than other more hidden, more *implicit* addictions. Yet explicit addictions are, basically, only symptoms of implicit addictions to deeper behavioral, emotional, and energetic patterns. However, *implicit pattern addiction*, even when life threatening, does not always signal its presence through explicit addictions. Implicit addiction can be very difficult to detect.

Pattern addiction is part of the human condition. It comes with the genetic package, which is supposedly survival oriented. So, should we concern ourselves with our hidden pattern addictions? Yes! This is the message here: The more prepared we are to detect and transcend detrimental behavior patterns—even and especially the hidden ones—to let them die, the more active a role we can play in our emotional, physical, and spiritual health, *and the more free will we will have.* There is no freedom without free will.

Most implicit pattern addictions are built over a long period of time. This is because most neurological programming—which involves the establishment of electrical or energetic patterns throughout the body—takes place over time. Such patterning becomes detrimental when harmful to the emotional, physical, and/or spiritual well-being of the individual (or family or community or society or planet). Pattern addiction frequently manifests itself in explicit symptoms such as the destructive addictions named above and also in physical pain, chronic ailments including ulcers, and possibly even diseases such as cancer.

Some pattern addiction is so subtle, so very implicit, that it involves holding patterns or blockages of necessary electrical charges and critical signals from the brain, and full blood flow, and ample oxygen, to remote parts of the body. By remote, we mean nerve endings, organs, brain cells, and other tissues of which we are often unaware, signifying distance from consciousness. The more aware we are of something, the closer we are to it, and to correcting it. Tight musculature surrounding digestive organs can interfere with the transmission of oxygen and neurological impulses involved in building or using digestive enzymes. Tight musculature in the head and neck can lead to jaw grinding. As Oriental medicine suggests, most afflictions are the product of energy flow disturbances. A rebalancing or correction in the transmission of neurological energy throughout the body can alleviate many problems. When this rebalancing occurs (often difficult to achieve until the process is learned), a harmful energetic pattern—the implicit pattern of the physical pain, the ulcer, the tumor, the drug addiction, the brainwashing—is broken. Without such a correcting of the underlying and more implicit pattern addictions, without the erasing of the programming behind the physical and psychological symptoms, the same or similar symptoms can continue, recur, and expand. This is, of course, due in part to the inability of current medical and psychological technology to do more.

DRUG ADDICTION AS AN EXAMPLE
Drug addiction offers one of the most tangible exam-

ples of patterning and some of the most tangible evidence that addiction to a pattern can be transcended. Drug addiction (we include alcohol in referring to drugs) is therefore a key, but not the only example in this book. You will see the parallels between drug addiction and all pattern addiction as you study the following pages. Study very carefully to see how these words apply to you, whether or not you have ever been drug-addicted.

Let's examine the societal implications of this threatening explicit addiction so common in modern times, and let's look for the broader message being relayed to our species by this addiction. Many illusions surround drug (and alcohol) addiction. One is the illusion of health. Far too many drug-addicted individuals are in a state of denial about their health problems. Too many claim that they are not addicted and use their seemingly good health as proof that they are not. But their lives are wounded. These people are operating under the *illusion* of health as well as under the *illusion* of not being addicted. Most people who suffer from any sort of pattern addiction are in a state of denial about its severity, if they admit its existence at all. This denial is often part of the programming.

This sort of programming affects everyone. It is not only the addicted individual who generates illusions; the social machinery does so as well. Look at the addiction treatment and beyond to the general medical communities—they operate under the *illusion* that addiction and

other "illnesses" require "treatment" and that the forms of
psychological and medical treatment provided are appropriate for treating explicit addictions and "illnesses."
Pattern addiction, however, is not a symptom that can be
medicated; it is not a tumor that can be cut out; it is not
a sickness that can be fully treated by traditional medical
practices. There are complex pattern addictions lurking
behind the drug addictions and other mental and physical illnesses medicine seeks to treat. Pattern addiction is a
crisis of the heart and soul *and will.* It is evidence of the
diminishment, the dying, of free will, and evidence of the
preordained submission to deep, preordained programming.

In this profound crisis of the heart, soul, and will, lies
the possibility of transformation, and of transcendence.
(*Transformation* and *transcendence* are not typical listings
in medical school curricula.) Crisis is an alarm, an alert,
an opportunity for attention. Most people wait for an
explicit alarm, for a major psychological or physical crisis,
to begin to even vaguely address their underlying pattern
addictions. For drug-addicted persons, this crisis is called
"hitting bottom." Hitting bottom can compel addicted or
otherwise afflicted individuals to seize the opportunity to
learn, and to care, about their mental, physical, and spiritual health, and about their effect upon the world they
live in. Hitting bottom is a call to action. Many people
who think that they have never been detrimentally pat-

tern addicted have not experienced this opportunity. Because the process of overcoming deep pattern addiction requires change on all levels, hitting bottom can actually provide a rare opportunity for profound personal change, and for the realization of our psychological, creative, and spiritual potentials.

Today, at least some members of the addiction treatment and general medical communities have come to understand this: The *crisis of addiction provides the opportunity for transformation.* Effective addiction treatment is not "warehousing" the unwanted or incompetent members of society. It is not "protecting sick people from themselves," or even "protecting society from sick people." It is important for the health care community (of which addiction treatment is a part) to recognize addiction and all forms of affliction as opportunities for transformation, and to seek to bring about that transformation. When addicted or ill individuals arrive at a treatment service, program, or other facility, they should find themselves at the door to mental, physical, and spiritual health—to a greater degree of free will and freedom. Only then will they stand on the threshold of *transcendence.* Only then can they bring about and "harvest" the death of the negative patterning they seek to be free from. And only then can they contribute to the welfare of all humanity.

All too often, addicted and otherwise afflicted individuals find themselves standing at a door to anything but

health. Drug treatment and most other health care services manifest a range of attitudes toward affliction, but
they rarely say, "Welcome. We are fortunate to have you
among us, because you are about to lead us in an exploration of the mind, body, and spirit. You are about to meet
the challenge of addiction to hidden patterning, to
understand the death of your patterning, and in that
understanding explore the frontiers of healing, of freedom, of human potential, and of the human soul. We are
truly fortunate to have you among us, leading the way to
liberation."

Instead, addicted people are stigmatized, frowned
upon, punished, or treated like "very sick people," and
very sick people are treated as society's unwanted, society's throw-aways. It is not so much a lack of expertise
that is the problem with most health care, but a lack of
understanding: understanding of what "sick" individuals
are all about and respect for the critical role that they can
play in the evolution of human consciousness and free
will. (See Chapter 11.)

WHY OUR CHEMICALIZATION
AND MECHANIZATION?

We have heard so much about "the drug problem" and
still we overlook its grim reality—the narcotization of
human life is upon us. Our robotization is here. Drug
abuse and addiction is the sign of crisis, not only for the

addicted individual, but for everyone in our society. We need to better understand this crisis, as it teaches us about what is happening to all of us. It signals the tensions emerging in two major areas of modern existence.

One tension is the problem of *chemicalization*. Slowly, man-made chemicals are filling our air, our water, our food, our bodies, and our brains. Our homes are cleaned with detergents. Plastics are everywhere—we wear them, we play with them, we even breathe them. Medicine offers chemical solutions to many of our health problems. A reliance on contrived chemicals has become a way of life in our modern world. As a result, we are all becoming chemically dependent. What a trap! What a paradox! Drug- and alcohol-addicted people, singled out as the only chemically dependent ones, are making the reality of everyone's increasing dependence on chemicals more apparent.

The second tension is caused by the problem of *mechanization*. Slowly, almost invisibly, we are surrendering our individual freedom. We are acquiescing to the reality of what we can call *"numbership,"* where we identify ourselves as a series of numbers (telephone, social security, driver's license, tax identification) and mechanical processes (checking in and checking out, registering, paying, driving). Without even seeing it happen, we are beginning to treat ourselves as machines. It is ironic that contained in the word *numbership* is the word *numb*. As we become more like machines, we actually become numb to our humanity. Programming overrides free will.

And here is the alarm going off: Many addicted individuals claim that they want to "numb the pain" of their existences by using drugs to "turn off." We are learning more about our switches; and we say that some of us are addicted to the chemical switches we call "drugs." It may be more than just some of us. Just about everyone has turned to painkillers to deal with headaches, body aches, and injuries. Check the inside of your medicine chest. Can you toss out its contents without hesitation?

Elaborate chemical switches are an increasing part of modern life. And so are electrical switches (such as television) and emotional switches (events we rely upon to change our feelings, such as parties for energy or happiness, music for sexual arousal or relaxation, holidays for escape or comfort, disagreements for anger or righteousness, full blown arguments for violence or tension release). As you can see from this partial list, the switches are not, in themselves, bad for us. It is the way we use them and the tendency we have to rely on them—to run on automatic—rather than paying attention to how we are turning events, emotions, objects, and chemicals into switches and ourselves into things that can be switched on and off.

Because of our shared dependence upon switches, we can see that the drug addiction treatment community has the opportunity to turn the social crises of chemicalization and mechanization into opportunities for everyone. If the treatment community can turn chemicalization and mechanization around in the individuals it treats, then it can make an impact on the societal level as well. Society is made up of individuals, some of whom manifest explicit addictions, and all of whom are subject to implicit addictions that may be harmful. Addiction treatment can become the door to individual *and* to societal health, especially if that treatment can expand to include implicit addiction. Some of this implicit pattern addiction will be the underlying cause of what medicine has been calling chronic and acute illness. We all must make way for a change of thought about all forms of what we call *disease,* and the medical community is no exception. Dis-ease is a symptom of deep and difficult to see pattern addiction. Our response to dis-ease must become far more subtle, more energy-oriented, and more intuitive.

HOW PATTERN ADDICTIONS CONTROL US

When a society, a globe full of societies, grows alarmed about drug trafficking, smuggling across borders, narcoterrorism, and drug addiction (as does ours from time to time), it is responding to explicit problems. And yet there is an unspoken, intuitive understanding of the implicit spiritual ramifications of such explicit problems. Something about the deepest level of the human condition is being expressed.

The problem of addiction goes much deeper than a simple lack of knowledge as to a "drug lord's" whereabouts or a failure of border closure. Chemical dependence is only one expression of a far more common and more harmful behavior that afflicts our society—destructive dependence. Anyone can fall into a destructive habit. Some people have a destructive dependence on food, others on sex, still others on the people in their close personal relationships—and some people have a destructive chemical dependence. The reality of human existence is that a "little addict person" lurks within, is implanted in, all of us. To better understand this little addict person we all share, let's consider two key concepts: *addictive materialism* and *addictive inadequacy*. These are most readily understood in cases of tangible addiction, because tangible or explicit addiction patterns are more easily traced than more subtle implicit patterns, which may or may not have overt physical expression.

Addictive materialism is pervasive. It binds most everyone to material reality. Think about materialism. One way to look at explicit addiction is to see drug-and/or object-addicted people as materialistic. They reach outside themselves for a material thing, a sort of mechanism—a car, house, television, computer, someone's body, food, or a drug—as a way of working with their psyches. For example, if they feel depressed, they may buy something, turn something on, or take a "drink," a "pill," a "hit," or a "line." They depend upon an external material item to rescue them from an undesired internal state of mind. Of course their state of mind may reflect external predicaments, but their ability to cope with those predicaments is not based on a continual process of interacting with them. Instead, it is naively based on taking or experiencing a concrete external item or object, as in a "pill" or "drink." The drug-addicted individual's particular preoccupation with a chemical substance is an obvious escape from the more arduous task of really dealing with feelings and situations. However, most people engineer escape in some parallel fashion. Drugs and other material things have become the "answer" for so many of us. In a materialistic society, we are conditioned to depend on a material substance or object or act in order to avoid the pain of actually living through and learning from a crisis. Such false escapes into materialism are not the route to freedom.

Compounding the problem of addictive materialism is addictive inadequacy. During the 1960s, young drug users claimed with great idealism that they were "turning on" and "raising" their consciousness through the use of mind-altering chemicals. A few decades later, it became clear that far too many of these untrained, unguided, users, perhaps without being aware of it, were actually trying to turn *off,* or to *diminish* their consciousnesses. This kind of user has come to rely on drugs (including

alcohol) to take the more jagged edges off the harsh
realities of life. In this picture of sacrilegious drug abuse
and addiction, individuals use drugs, but not for mind-
expansion and spiritual growth. These individuals use
drugs because they cannot cope with reality. Their psychological coping mechanisms are insufficient and inadequate in the face of the pressures of modern life. Most of
us are taught very few adequate coping skills as we grow
up in this society. Over time, we become addicted to our
inadequacies, our inabilities to cope with life. This
addictive inadequacy becomes deeply hidden unless an
explicit addiction brings it out. If chemically addicted
individuals have learned any coping skills early on in life,
they lose them through disuse when they handicap themselves with the artificial coping mechanisms of alcohol
and other drugs, and other objects of addiction. We all
allow our coping skills to atrophy in a similar fashion.
Material reality offers us many false crutches to lean on.

THESE ADDICTIONS APPLY TO ALL OF US

Addictive materialism and addictive inadequacy:
These two explanations point to the global nature of pattern addiction. The problems of addictive materialism
(dependence on outer means for solving inner problems)
and of addictive inadequacy (allowing internal coping
mechanisms to be inadequate) are common to a greater
portion of society than the mere population of those

addicted to chemicals. How many of us go shopping and end up overspending when we are bored, depressed, or faced with a crisis? How many of us use a relationship to escape knowing ourselves? How many of us overeat to avoid feeling? How many of us avoid doing our real work by occupying ourselves with gossip and trivia? How many of us have trouble dealing with the realities of life and are forced to depend on material externalities? Not all of us are addicted to dangerous chemicals, but we all exhibit signs of addictive materialism and addictive inadequacy. We all regularly seek to compensate for these addictive characteristics within ourselves. We all have a great deal in common. If we are honest with ourselves we will admit that we have seen the pattern addict. And he, or she, is us.

HOW WE FORM PATTERN ADDICTIONS

What you do here, in your physical dimension, has effects far beyond the reality you see and know. *Pattern addictions, whatever their symptoms, trap energy.* Be careful how you use your energy, whether it is your physical, your emotional, your financial, or your spiritual energy. Try to see the patterns you are forming and feeding.

Pattern addictions sneak up on people. Take, for example, the development of a drug dependence, or a relationship dependence, or any other explicit addiction. These standard addictions do not begin explicitly. You may even be in a troubled pattern addiction right now and not realize it because it is not yet an explicit addiction. Look at what it is that you think you are doing quite casually. An addiction to a drug or a specific behavior usually begins with *casual behavior.* Casual behavior is light, experimental, seemingly without deep consequences. The experimenter lives in a society that appears to allow at least some degree of freedom to experiment and explore. "Try this just once . . . then decide if you want to try it again." Or, "I dare you to try this. Come on, show us what a man (or woman) you are." Experimenting is a part of growing up, and of living in what we think is a "free" country. But unfortunately, too much casual behavior becomes *regular behavior.*

Casual Behavior ⎯⎯⎯⎯▶ Regular Behavior

At some point, some regular behaviors become a bit too regular. The regular behavior, if in some way detrimental, can then become a troubled behavior.

Regular Behavior ⎯⎯⎯⎯▶ Troubled Behavior

People who are exhibiting *troubled behavior* continue to do so in the face of adverse effects to themselves (their health, their minds, their work), their families, their businesses, their neighborhoods, or their societies. It is easy to slip from regular behavior to troubled behavior because the early signs of troubled behavior are subtle and often go undetected.

Again, consider drug use for a blatant example. Someone who has a few drinks at a bar on the way home from work is already driving "under the influence"— however slight that influence may seem. Of course, driving home may be entirely possible. The point is that many users who are in a state of troubled behavior do not consider the risks that their use are posing to themselves or to others. And, they are not aware of how easily they can slip from regular to troubled behavior and then into full blown addicted behavior. And this highly predictable chain of descent into pattern addiction is typical of all addictions, not just drug addiction.

Casual→ Regular→ Troubled→ Addicted Behavior

Fortunately, not everyone who tries alcohol or other drugs, or overeating, or gambling, or theft, or a violent relationship, travels this tragic path. Some of these persons, these casual behavers, try a behavior once and then consider the experiment completed. But all too commonly, casual behavers unwittingly slip into regular behavior. We confidently tell ourselves, "It can't happen to me. I'm too much in control of my life to develop an addiction to anything, whether it be a drug, a thing, a person, or an activity. I'm just having a little fun or exploring a possibility." In reality, we are deluding ourselves. Case history after case history demonstrates that casual behavior, without the training in how to avoid programming ourselves, dramatically increases the probability of developing a fully addictive behavior. And any behavior conducted regularly increases the chances of its being programmed into our bodies and brains.

This is an explanation of the descent into detrimental pattern addiction. Any behavior can be expressed once or twice. But somehow we are blind to the crossing of the boundaries between casual and regular, regular and troubled, troubled and addicted. Why? Because we are genetically programmed to slip, unaware, into pattern addition.

THE FREEING AND RIGHT USE OF OUR ENERGY

Is this genetic programming mere happenstance? Is it the misfiring of the survival-oriented function (designed to have us respond to red lights and the other safety signals automatically)? Or are we prisoners of a mechanism buried, implanted, deep within our coding—a mechanism rendering us readily programmed creatures of habit?

We have allowed ourselves to believe that our programming function is a necessary part of our descension into material reality; however, it is not. The challenge is to remain free while living in easily programmable physicality. We have to know when and how to allow our programmings—our robot selves—to die in order for us to remain free. And we must be the constant monitors of our energies. In their right use our energies support free will. Trapped in programmed loops, our energies are imprisoned.

F I V E DEATH AND TRANSCENDENCE

Breaking a pattern is dying. Are you prepared to die? Are you prepared to release old patterns? Are you ready to transcend? Will you succeed? Can you die well?

We become addicted to the very programming we would shed in death. Thus we resist this shedding. But, when this shedding—the death of a pattern—finally takes place, it is a healing event.

TRANSCENDING YOUR PROGRAMMING

To die well, to bring about a worthwhile living death, you must break your addiction to the programming that controls the pattern you want to break. Those concerned about chemical dependence, painful relationship patterns, chronic pain, life-threatening diseases, and other crises of programming are working with the same question: How can I break out of my addiction to this programming? What type of death will I require to release, to free, myself? The only difference between the obvious and the more hidden pattern addictions is that some addictions to programming are more subtle than others. The drug-addicted individual sees a physical thing, a drug, to which he or she is addicted. Individuals dealing with repeated emotional or physical health patterns often have no physical objects onto which they can project or externalize their patterns, which makes the problem-process of addiction to their programming much more difficult to see, far more implicit.

The first step in transcending is to face the reality that addiction to patterns takes place in all of us. Explicit addictions serve as great learning vehicles. They make the hidden components of pattern addiction much more apparent to us. Implicit addictions are frequently discovered by people who are in recovery from explicit addictions or who are fighting serious physical illnesses. These individuals become examples for all of us. They lead the way through the matrix of death into the realm of transcendence.

CONDITIONS FOR TRANSCENDENCE
Whether or not it is physical, healthy death involves transcendence, one of the most special experiences we can

have during a lifetime. Transcendence is life healing.

Many of our problems are actually encountered or created to provide us with the opportunity to transcend them, to heal our lives. As human beings we have a choice. We can either become so overwhelmed by our problems that we miss out on this amazing opportunity, or we can realize that pattern addiction is a *potential-laden* situation.

Those who are addicted to a pattern (whether drug use or eating or something more subtle, such as an emotional or energetic pattern) have a wonderful opportunity to experience transcendence—specifically to transcend pattern addiction. Transcendence requires a new outlook on a situation. No matter how bleak and painful a situation may appear, it can be changed by being *reperceived.* This means that, before any changes can occur, you must be convinced of the fact that *you can turn things around!* You must believe in the possibility of transcendence. You must also understand the phases and process of transcendence, which must be studied continually. No matter what level of understanding you reach, there is always more to be learned.

Remember, there is no such thing as a free lunch. Transcendence is hard work. The transcendence process requires *your commitment, your attention, your fortitude,* and *your faith in the process.* These are interactive states of mind.

Phases of Transcendence

Transcendence is a continuous process through which an individual achieves elevation to higher spiritual planes, where she or he experiences greater awareness and a higher degree of freedom. Transcendence is composed of four profound phases, each of which is necessary for the process. These phases of transcendence are:

Phase 1: Struggle
Phase 2: Paradox
Phase 3: Insight
Phase 4: Spiritual Elevation

Each phase has its own special characteristics. You will find diagrams of these phases as they are discussed in the following pages. As you examine each diagram, try to think of your life in terms of it. Make these diagrams part of your own mental imagery. Draw them again and again. Drawing simple pictures of complex ideas often helps to learn about them on a deeper level.

Phase 1: Struggle. Every day we struggle—with other people, with family relationships, with work relationships, with ourselves, with morality, and maybe also with our cravings for drugs, with balancing our checkbooks, with heavy traffic, with our health, with our tempers, with our moods, with living up to some internal or

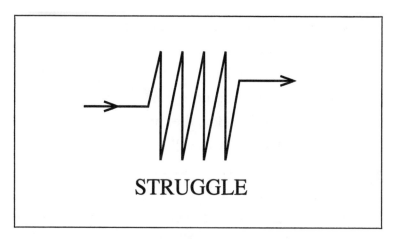

STRUGGLE

Figure 5.1 Phase 1: Struggle

external standard. We often struggle without recognizing or seeing beyond the struggle, being so deeply caught up that it becomes impossible to step back and say, "Oh, I am struggling. This must be the first phase of transcendence." But it is just this observation that will set us on the path to transcendence. When we *are* struggling we must take the time to tell ourselves that *we are struggling*—and that this is good, because it is the first phase of transcendence.

Study Figure 5.1. This pattern illustrates the ups and downs, pushes and pulls, and highs and lows so typical of the struggling phase. During a true struggle, there must be low points in order for there to be high points—both extremes are integral to it.

Phase 2: Paradox. Paradox is a catalytic experience. It

can be painful. It can be frightening. It can be deadly. It can produce a zombie-like effect in those who experience it. Paradox is the experience of being in a situation from which there seems to be no escape, no resolution. The more powerful the paradox, the more a trap it feels, the greater the release from it will be. Energy trapped in paradox builds a valuable tension, unless it is trapped too long. Then it stagnates and weakens and the person in the deteriorating paradox is powerlessly and permanently trapped with no energy left for release.

Sometimes parents submit children to paradoxes in the form of double binds something like this: "Which coat do you like?" a parent may ask a child. "The red coat or the blue one?" When the child says, "The red coat," the parent says, "That's not a good choice, you should like the blue one." And when the child says, "The blue one," the parent says, "Well, the red one is much better." When this happens, the child is experiencing a double bind: Lose-Lose. In this case, there is nothing the child can do that would elicit a positive response from the parent. The child is bound by unpleasant consequence no matter which choice he or she makes. There is no escape. The situation holds, or so it would seem, no real choices.

Some double binds come from outside us but most come from within because we allow ourselves to feel them as double binds. In living their lives, both children and adults create double bind situations for themselves with or without the help of other people. For the child above, release from the bind is seeing the folly of the parent's reasoning and not taking it personally. This is a large job for a child.

One double bind that many people find themselves in is chemical dependence. When we repeatedly take a drug to escape a painful, stressful, or boring situation, the situation we are trying to escape becomes even more painful, stressful, or boring each time we return to it, coming "down" from the trip. While no escape is no escape, the drug escape is also no escape.

Paradoxes like this are extremely stressful and often painful. But faith in the transcendence process shows us that paradox serves a purpose. Without the tension, the feeling of being trapped in an unwinnable situation, there is no impetus for release, for moving on, for growing. The tension created by paradoxes, when used well, can generate enough energy to break out of them. We must learn to spot paradoxes before they stagnate in order to harvest the valuable energy from them. Without the painful tenseness of paradox, we cannot experience the release—the jump or shift in perception—that is produced by breaking out of the paradoxical double bind.

Paradox is illustrated in Figure 5.2. Study it for a few minutes. It shows the "standoff" or "holding pattern" in which people get caught or trap themselves. They need to let something of themselves die and to experience tran-

Figure 5.2 Phase 2: Paradox

scendence. The only way out of this holding pattern is to break out of it and move on, to increase perception to see beyond the limits of the entrapping double bind. The two arrows ending up against each other and going nowhere represent the forces that hold a pattern-addicted person in his or her trap. One force (one arrow) is the powerful tendency to stay stuck, to stay pattern addicted, to avoid change at all costs. The other force (the other arrow) is the stressful and painful effect of actually using excuses or drugs or relationships or objects to forget stress and escape pain and ending up with less sense of escape than ever. This deadlock can hold us in its grip indefinitely. Or, if we choose to truly escape it, to really transcend it, to let the paradox die, it can provide a take-off point into another level of awareness and a healing.

As has been explained, when the paradox of pattern addiction explodes, energy is released. That fantastic energy can bring profound insight when harvested. Whatever our pattern addictions may be, we can harness the energy found in their paradoxes and then move—fast forward—into transcendence of that paradox. To do so, we must become highly alert to any paradoxical, locked-in, tensions we feel and to whatever implicit pattern addictions generate them.

Phase 3: Insight. Insight is a profound experience. But it comes in small, short-lived packages. Sometimes we experience it without even realizing it. We may be driving along and suddenly grasp something about a problem that has been bothering us. Or we may be working—perhaps on a relationship or household or scientific or construction problem—and suddenly glimpse an unexpected solution. All at once a new idea comes to mind. We suddenly discover a new way of looking at a problem. We are enlightened for a moment. This is an insight.

Insight is illustrated graphically in Figure 5.3. Look at

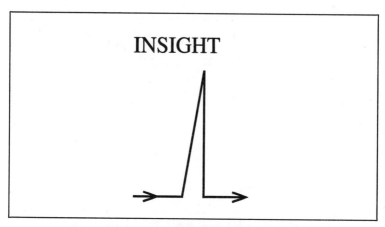

Figure 5.3 Phase 3: Insight

the figure for a while. It suggests the glimpse, or perception, of another way of seeing the world and of being in the world. The highest point in this diagram is this flash of realization. It represents a peek (and a peak) into a higher level of experience. Now notice that the line falls back, or almost back, to its original level. This is because insight is a temporary jump in perception. It does not automatically bring growth. In order to grow, insight must be recognized and sustained. When it is, spiritual elevation becomes reality.

Phase 4: Spiritual Elevation. Spiritual elevation is illustrated in Figure 5.4. Gaze at it. What does this diagram symbolize to you? This pattern signifies a jump in perception. This jump is actually an insight that is *sustained.* The self, the soul, the spirit, rises to a new level of being and maintains it. This "holding on" is best

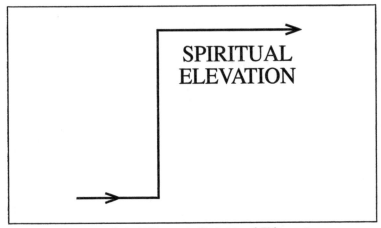

Figure 5.4 Phase 4: Spiritual Elevation

described as the experience of sustained insight. Without being sustained, the insight is usually bright and brief, dropping back to or close to the original, pre-insight, way of seeing and being in the world, as in Figure 5.3. Spiritual elevation differs from insight in that there is no going back to previous perceptions.

From the new level of being that is achieved by spiritual elevation, each of the phases of transcendence may have to be repeated in order to reach the next level of spiritual elevation. We can always discover new struggles, paradoxes, and insights to generate further spiritual growth.

This exciting and adventurous process of transcendence is suggested in Figure 5.5. It shows the four phases of transcendence linked together. The cycle of these

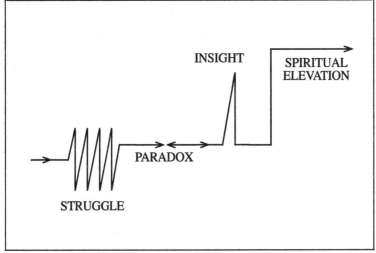

Figure 5.5 The Four Phases of Transcendence

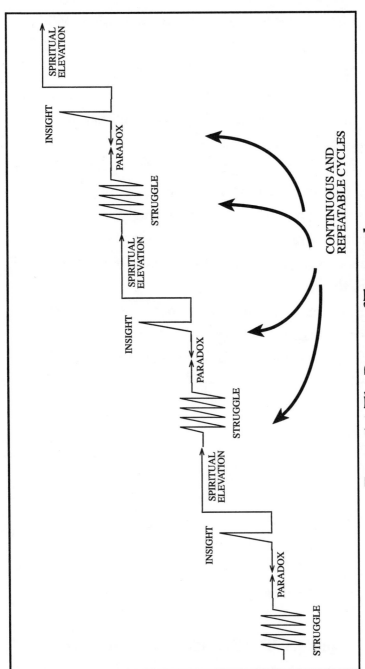

Figure 5.6 The Process of Transcendence

phases is repeatable, as in Figure 5.6. Contemplate these diagrams for a while.

Be certain that you understand that each phase may take barely a few seconds or may last for years. Some people struggle all their lives. Others live in a perpetual state of paradox. Some rotate between struggle and paradox, as Figure 5.7 demonstrates. Perhaps these people reach spiritual elevation at physical death. Some people have insights but do not recognize or sustain them; thus they continuously return to the same old paradox that produced these insights.

Each of us follows our own life pattern. However, no one's pattern is written in stone. If we were taught as children to recognize the four basic phases of transcendence, then it would be much easier for us, as adults, to see where we are in the process and to take conscious control of it. But no matter how old we are, we can always learn to harness the precious energy produced in each phase in order to move on to the next phase. We can learn to see our struggles as fertile ground for astounding growth. We can learn to appreciate paradox, recognize insight, and strive for spiritual elevation.

If you keep trying to see these four basic patterns in your life you will eventually understand that you are already on the path of transcendence. The gifts of life and death will then be clear to you. Your struggles are important stepping stones. Respect your struggles.

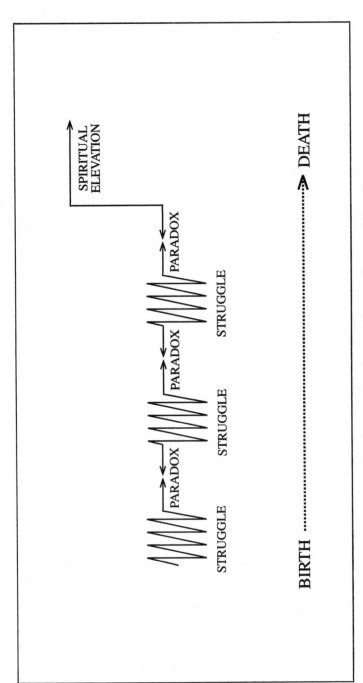

Figure 5.7 Rotation between Struggle and Paradox

Basic Ideas for Transcending Patterning

We have been examining the concept of transcendence—what it is, and what it takes to achieve it. The concept can be applied to any obstacle or difficulty we encounter, whether it be emotional, financial, physical, or another type of problem. Remember, even chronic and serious illnesses have pattern addiction components requiring transcendence. Even the experience of physical death can be viewed as an integral part of the ongoing and ever-inspiring transcendence process.

You can make this knowledge your own by reviewing the following basic ideas and then returning to the figures included in this chapter.

Idea One. Addiction to a pattern is a powerful bondage that can only be broken by something more powerful. We must accept this as a fact and appreciate the size and seriousness of the task of breaking pattern addiction.

Idea Two. Whether or not we exhibit any explicit addictions, we all are pattern addicts. Pattern addiction can be very subtle and difficult to recognize. Therefore some individuals either present themselves, or are presented, with the challenge of an explicit addiction so that they may recognize how addicted to patterning we all are. They then undergo the struggle to break out of their most explicit addictive patterns and in the process of that struggle, they experience growth. Some people have found the recognition of addiction to be their primary opportunity for growth. Drug, alcohol, food, gambling, and relationship addictions are some of the easiest patterns to spot and thus offer some of the most accessible opportunities to practice transcendence and to grow.

Idea Three. The ultimate form of learning is transcendence, a process composed of four phases: struggle, paradox, insight, and spiritual elevation. This pattern is a repetitive, never-ending process. Your entire experience of living and of dying large and small deaths is transformed the moment you identify the phase of the process you are currently experiencing.

Idea Four. One way to promote insight, spiritual elevation, and thus transcendence, is by fully experiencing the pain, struggle, and paradox of pattern addiction. Pattern-addicted individuals often *select* their particular expressions of addiction—their explicit addictions—and they select the intensities of their particular struggles and paradoxes to alert themselves to and set themselves free from their deeper addictions.

Idea Five. Remember that the transcendence described is a process that gains power as it progresses. Progressive transcendence can overcome pattern addiction and then, with focus, move beyond to awesome levels of enlightenment. There is no end point to this process.

Idea Six. Work to maintain the insights and spiritual elevations gained in the process of transcendence.

Idea Seven. With every full cycle of transcendence comes an entirely new way of seeing the self and the world. Be ever ready and open to dying, to total change, and to new life.

Only total change and an ongoing commitment to transcendence will heal the stifling wounds to the soul that are caused by the narcotization and robotization of detrimental pattern addiction. And only massive transcendence will heal and free the world. As the human species becomes more aware of its ability to consciously choose to transcend—escape—the trap of patterning in the physical world, it will ascend to the realm of the spirit. Conscious and focused biological death is not the only means of such ascendance; however, it is perhaps the most profound of all.

MAPPING YOUR DEATHS

S
I
X

Notice where you are and how you feel. Find yourself in the process of living and dying. Can you map your life? Can you map any of your living deaths? How about the roads leading up to those deaths?

RECOGNIZE THE FORK IN THE ROAD

There are times when life brings you to a fork in the road. Sometimes you don't see the fork coming. It just appears. Sometimes you don't realize that the fork has appeared, or that you are straddling the forked roads and feeling the imbalancing tug of conflicting choices.

When you feel substantially unsettled for a significant chunk of time (whatever that may be to you), take a look under your feet. Try to see where you are in your life. There, a choice to go one way or another—to take one

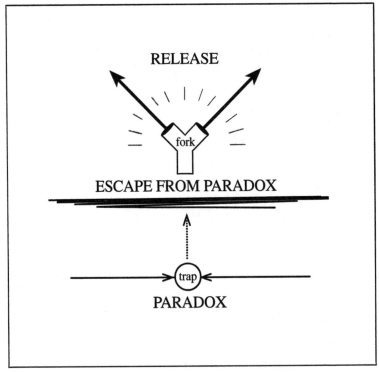

Figure 6.1 Escape from Paradox

course of action or another—must be made. Something must be left behind, no matter how painful.

Despite the anguish you may feel at having to make a choice, you can rejoice because you are actually at the junction we can call the "escape from paradox." Figure 6.1 shows energy trapped in a paradox, in a double bind, moving toward release in the "fork," and released in the "escape."

How do you move ahead now? Force yourself into a

commitment to go one way or the other. It is time to consciously and clearly choose to go further with the developments already forming in the fork or to choose to go back to the illusion of the safer, "saner" life within the paradox. This sounds odd, but it is actually less work to stay trapped than to break out. However, once out, you are much freer.

UNDERSTAND THE SENSE OF INSTABILITY

As you move toward escape from paradox, you may feel intensely unsettled. Either you or the world around you may seem chaotic, out of order. You may have no sense that things will ever look quite the same again. And you know that if you commit to escape, things will indeed never look the same again.

And so, as you move toward the change, toward your growth and survival, you destabilize your trap, you beat at the doors of your paradox. Things do become highly unstable. It is exactly this state of instability that any system, including that of a living organism (such as you), has to reach to evolve beyond its present level of development.

But what finally opens, loosens, an extremely rigid trap? The more rigid it is, the more energy is required to hold it in place. Some kind of psychophysical shock, a catastrophe, a small or large calamity, is usually required to loosen up a rigid system. Time for personal apocalypse.

HEAR YOUR VOICE

Become more sensitive to the subtle inputs you give yourself as you get ready to let a part of your life die. Pay attention to very quiet hints, murmurs in your mind that you would normally have missed or totally ignored. These inputs may contribute to your seeming to be unbalanced, in that you feel rather disturbed or crazy. But fear not. You are right where you should be.

About the time the tension crescendos, you may, if you listen, hear a voice in your head. Do not be alarmed. It will not harm you. This is your higher self talking, speaking to you from the dimensions beyond, from a place past now.

When you hear a voice guiding you, know that this is not craziness, not psychosis. You are transducing, reducing the frequency of the transmissions from your higher, wiser self to a frequency that your mind can receive. As you gain control over your receiving mechanisms, your instability will be increasingly unnecessary. You will consciously pick up a wider band of information from yourself and the world around you.

This widening of your band of perception is a marvelous advancement in the evaluation of your self, your consciousness, your soul. Still, at first, if you are sensitive enough and willing enough to hear your own voice, you may question or even deny the experience. This is not surprising. Such evolution, especially to those poor souls who have not been instructed in the process, can be excruciatingly disorienting. To help you with this, you are now being instructed in an introductory, subtle, and gentle manner. The excruciation may fade before the disorientation does. However, eventually both will become manageable and recede.

MAPS

As you undergo any transition, make yourself a map. If you cannot visualize well, then draw the map and keep it handy. Be ready to revise or add on to the map as you continue into the journey you have begun.

The following maps represent dying processes, both living deaths and physical deaths. These maps are for you to explain to yourself. This is your own teaching. Study these. Attempt to describe a process of change, of transition, of dying that fits each map. Then think of a few major changes you have experienced in your life, and map (on paper as well as in your mind) the process of leading up to, moving through, and leaving each of these transitions. Then draw a map of your present condition.

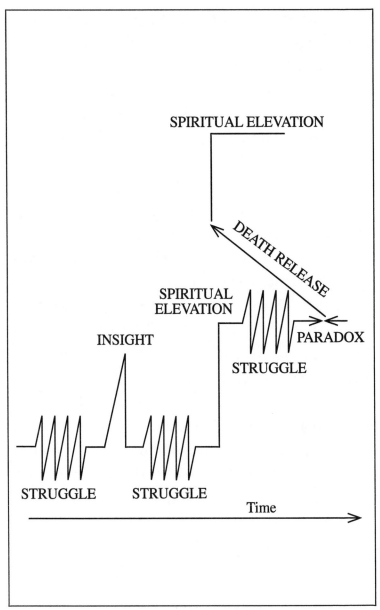

Figure 6.2 A Death Map

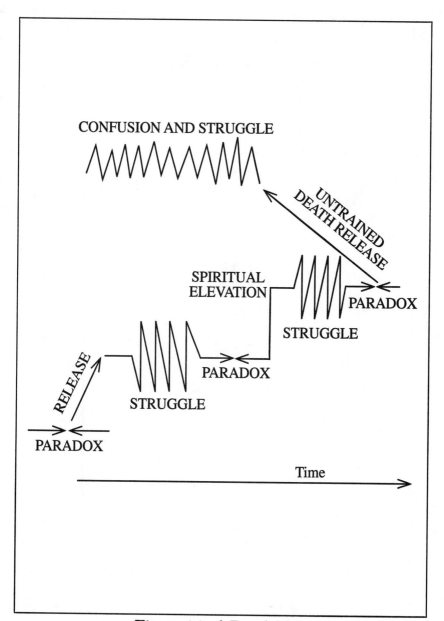

Figure 6.3 A Death Map

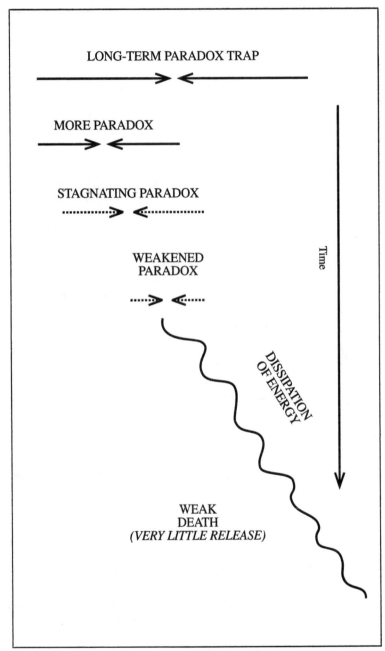

Figure 6. 4 A Death Map

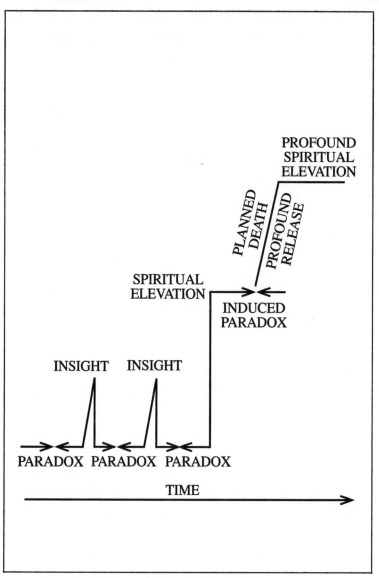

Figure 6. 5   A Death Map

When you construct your own map, try to include as many struggles, paradoxes, insights, and elevations as you have, are, or will be experiencing.

MASTERING TRANSITIONS FROM ONE DIMENSION OF REALITY TO ANOTHER

SEVEN

This little book asks you to take in and pull together some ancient and some modern teachings. Some of this material is a rethinking of medicine and psychology, some of it is a slightly different perspective on politics. Other parts of this material come from what is called "esoteric" teaching. Esoteric is defined as teaching reserved for the select few, the "eso-" or inner circle. It is considered the opposite of exoteric, that being teaching watered down for the many, for the "exo-" or outer circle. Why water down what you have a right to know?

WHY THIS ESOTERIC DISCUSSION?

You are being asked to rethink death because you are a far more potent being than most teachers of history, science, and religion have told you. You are so expansive a being that your energy field already touches many states of reality, many arrangements of energy, many dimensions. In fact, you are in contact with all dimensions at once, right here.

Right Here? You might wonder where else you could really be while you are right here. "Right here" is an elusive concept, although it sounds concrete to you. In reality, there is no more of a "right here" here than there is anywhere else. Basically, the sense of location you have is colored by your tie to your physical reality. This is only one dimension of existence. There are many other dimensions or arrangements of energy. Those dimensions are already all "right here." This is true because you, everyone of you, exist in a matrix of dimensions with varying degrees of physical and nonphysical reality.

Many of you are now asking why you cannot see these other dimensions. The answer is that you can see them, but not the way you usually see things. You will see much more when you learn to stop using your physical eyes as the ultimate arbiters of reality, when you retrain your optic nerve and develop your third eye to see beyond the material plane, to see outside linear time, and to see semi-material and nonmaterial essences as well as the physicality your eyes presently accept as real. Everything is right here whether or not you can see it right now. When your optic nerve learns to register a broader range of impulses and your brain finally accepts these as real, you will see what is here. This higher vision is detailed in a forthcoming book.

THE DIMENSIONS OF REALITY

Everyday life has many faces. Even within the limited realities in which many of us live, there are many realities. Energy is always arranging and rearranging.

Take some time to think—to let the concept become a part of you—of death as a transition or relocation of energy from one reality to another, or from one dimension of reality to another. You can make such a transition or relocation of energy with confidence and clarity, whatever the level of transition may be, whether it is a transition out of a relationship, out of a drug addiction, out of an illness, or out of a physical body in the case of biological death. Think of all your changes as being shifts from one state of reality to another.

The following discussion will help loosen any rigid perceptions of reality that may keep you from knowing this. Allow the ideas to flow into your mentality without working at taking them in. Remember that this discussion is basically telling you that you can learn to consciously rearrange your energy. You can break any energy pattern or formation in which you are trapped.

Use your imagination to practice changing your energy formation. See yourself shrinking down and passing through what feels to the mind to be something like the

eye of a needle and then expanding right into the relief of
what may seem to be heaven. You can come and go from
that heaven, to and from that sort of hyperspace, to and
from other dimensions, other vibrational levels of reality,
any time you choose. It is your right to be able to move
your imagination, your mind, your soul, your self, around
this way.

This passing through is one way to survive a calamity. In a passage that may feel like death, you decompose
your formation and pass right through the so-called eye
of the needle, the portal, into another dimension. In fact,
calamity, or apocalypse, whether it is an apocalypse that is
all in your mind, a terminal illness, or a natural disaster
such as an intense earthquake, or something more massive than that, is often the reason for reaching through
the eye toward the beyond. The beyond is simply a place
where your energy can be free of the detrimental patterns,
the rigid energy formations, trapping it.

MOVING THROUGH THE DIMENSIONS

Recall the earlier discussion of how important it is to
know when you are at a fork in the road. It is equally
important to be able to find these passages, these needles'
eyes or portals, these windows into other realities. They
are all around you but remain hidden until you train yourself to see them.

With practice, you will find your windows. Yes, they

really are windows of opportunity although, if you can spot them at all, they may appear, at first, to be difficult-to-access escape hatches. You can move through these windows by imagining that move, or by actually making that move. You can become either very, very small or compact, or so very spread out and vast that you have no physical density. Remember that you can see yourself becoming very dense—into a sort of nowhereness—or spread very thin—into a sort of everywhereness. It is your choice, at any moment, with any degree of belief you choose, to employ these formation-shifting techniques. Just think yourself into the form you choose. Imagination is quite powerful in this way.

Moving from one dimension of reality to another is a form of death. All death, including living death in which there is no physical death, can be compared to this process. The experience will vary depending on your preparation for it. Learn to recognize the sensations that accompany the formation-shifting of death. You may feel you are traveling through sheets of glass, shattering each of them as you move, then being propelled by the force of that shattering still deeper through the glass sheets, which continue to shatter as you proceed. You may feel as if you are suffocating, drowning for a while, as if you are trapped on the bottom of a lake or sea. The suffocation may be intense if you let fear take over, with your lungs feeling compressed to complete flatness. You may feel blind, think you cannot see anything.

If you find yourself in the midst of such an experience, let time pass. After a while, you may see flat slabs of light fly out of the dark, like pieces of broken glass. Imagine that you become one of those pieces of broken glass. *Let yourself shatter.* Feel that you are breaking apart from your holding pattern, from your structure. If you feel no relief when you shatter, if you still feel compressed to suffocating flatness, hang in there. Let yourself be flat—but take on a fluidity to your flatness: Sense that you are trapped in the surface of a body of water, the top of a lake or sea.

You are formation-shifting, and, in this case, accepting your reduction to a two-dimensional form (or state of mind) for a while. During this time, remember this description. You will know that the intense flatness, the compression you feel, is merely a passing state (unless you choose to stay in that compressed form). This compression can feel like tension, claustrophobia, or numbness.

Should you have such an experience, you (your consciousness and your essence) are indeed passing through the flatness, the reduction, of two-dimensional reality, where everything exists on a plane. But, even as this is happening to you, you may cling to your earthly views of reality. You may have no sense that you are compressing in order to launch yourself. In terms of cross-dimensional travel, you can say that you are launching yourself from the third dimension into the second in order to move into the fourth and escape a tension or danger, a physical (or emotional) catastrophe in the third. You may do this dimension-hopping, this form of dying, instinctively. However, it is best for you to do this consciously.

If you find yourself in imaginary or actual darkness, wait. Remember that a magnificent stream of glistening light will eventually wash through the dark flatness. Ride this light. When you feel air, or something like air, rush into your lungs, you will realize with relief that you are not exactly dead. Instead, you have just traveled across dimensions. You have just crossed one or more thresholds. You have just disintegrated and reorganized your energy. Your old formation, your patterning, may have died; you have survived.

TIME OR DIMENSIONAL TRAVEL

Remember that these journeys require you to use your imagination and to believe in, to convince your essence of, what you are doing.

In the previous experience, you allowed your essence to become a reflection—just a flat reflection of your three-dimensional self. Becoming flat, two dimensional, is one way to move into the fourth dimension, where time travel is the typical form of motion—the way travel around town or around the planet is typical three-dimensional travel. The third dimension, the material plane, is centrally located, in terms of density, among all the dimensions of reality. If you want to make a basic but strong move up a dimension, to move around in time, either backward or forward, you can "aim." Just move your energy down a dimension, as if you are pulling back on a sling shot. If you do this right, you can return from time travel back to the third dimension with your body intact and even with the clothes you had on when you left. If you choose to.

Or you can alter your physical condition by working on your energy arrangements while in a higher, less physical dimension. Later, if you choose to again become more dense, more physical, you will be changed. This raising of energy to a higher frequency, a less dense form, allows for rearrangements, restructurings, and healings that can then be moved back down to the physical plane. This process will be detailed in a later volume.

Know the Dimensions of Energy

As you master the use of your energy, and raise the power of your consciousness, you will have more ability to navigate all your deaths and transitions. Mastering the dying process—or transitional passage—makes life very worth living. In fact, *only when death is mastered is life lived.*

To master death, you must know dimensions. Basically, the dimensions are a rainbow of realities, with the most dense reality at one end and the least dense at the other. Try to visualize the basic geometry of the basic dimensions. First, there is the dimensionless point, the zero dimension. A point, when extended, forms a line, a row of points. This line represents the first dimension because it has only one dimension—length. When you drag that line through space, you get a row of lines, or a plane. This plane is the second dimension because it has only two dimensions, length and width. When you drag this plane through space, you get something with depth. Now the length and width of the plane also have depth, the way a cube does. This is thus three-dimensional reality, which you know well. This is where you hold your physical body.

Living in a physical body, one which ages over time, you exist on the border of the third and fourth dimensions. Any three-dimensional life form moving through time is to some degree traveling in the fourth dimension. But the agility of that life form's travel is hampered by its ties to its third-dimensional structure, the body in which it lives. Nevertheless, even the body can be a vehicle for multidimensional travel. If you move that physical form rapidly enough, faster than the speed of light for example, it transforms to something far less dense. Its energy formation is transformed: it "dies."

Mastering death involves understanding multidimensional reality. Let's look at the mental shift involved in moving your energy from one reality to another. What are the higher vibrational levels your energy can attain? Know that dimensions above your material dimension of reality progress geometrically as do the point, the line, the plane, and the three-dimensional object. Certainly, it is difficult for many of us to see the progression beyond the dimension or condition of reality we know best, which is for you three-dimensional reality. But this becomes easier with practice.

Move the three-dimensional object, the cube, through time, with its length, width, and depth each moving through time in its own direction, and you have an incredible expansion! This is the *time burst* typical of the full fourth-dimensional energy expansion. This time burst signifies the LEAP into the fourth dimension. A LEAP is a movement from one dimension to the next. A LEAP is usually best and most efficiently brought about when consciously constructed. This LEAP is, of course, a death, as each shift in dimension or in reality is a death. The more trained the dying being is, the cleaner the death LEAP. You can master this LEAP and use it anytime you wish.

Now take that energy expansion, that time burst, that LEAP, and raise it yet another level. Do not think about this too hard. Just let your mind *review the nature of the mental shift* that is needed to go from the idea of a point to the idea of a line or a straight piece of thread; from the idea of a line to the idea of a plane or a flat piece of paper;

from the idea of a plane to the idea of a cube or any object; from the idea of an object to the idea of that object or body aging, expanding, or bursting out in all directions in a rapid evaporation of itself. Each mental shift across a dimensional barrier is a LEAP.

Now, with the understanding of the mental shift it takes to think about the movement from one dimension of geometry to another, you can begin to fathom a much higher dimension. Take that rapidly burst evaporating essence and move it to a place beyond time as you know it, where everything is present and abundant at every moment, where light streams look like slow rivers beneath you. This is where the high resonance of energies produces a very clear sensation, best described as the purest, highest love in the Cosmos, love that fills and becomes your essence. This is the wondrous fifth dimension. Here you can indeed see and "feel" the essence of the Cosmos, and the perfect meshing of its most basic components. You see light moving in and out of time, forming and unforming, appearing and disappearing, slowing down and speeding up, moving in and out of lower dimensions. These light waves are rivers of energy running through realities. You can learn to ride them, again allowing your imagination to teach you.

The death process, when it entails leaving the physical body, can cast a person unaware into this fifth dimension. To stay conscious and navigate your journey for yourself, divorce yourself from any overwhelming amazement at the beauty you find there. If and when you see entire gigantic galaxies and tiny subatomic particles all at the same time, unaided by telescope or microscope, stay focused on your self. The profound surprise of such perception tends to dissolve many spirits. If you choose to dissolve at this point, make this a clear and conscious choice. You will be aware that you have no physical body, but you will nevertheless feel your life force and any excitations of it. The divine exhilaration, the ecstasy, you will feel is like being wildly in love, but millions of times more intense. If you do stay conscious here and choose not to dissolve, you will feel with absolute certainty that you are still your own essence. You will take the form of a massive, but massless, body of energy.

If and when you dissolve, you will move from this ecstatic fifth dimension to the omnipresent, all-knowing, all-being, everywhere sixth dimension. (We will call this complex dimensional level simply "the sixth" for teaching purposes.) This is the Oneness. Only if you consciously enter the Oneness, the sixth dimension, can you return from it at will. The Oneness is the unveiled, always present, very clear awareness that you are connected to all that exists throughout the Cosmos. When you enter the sixth dimension, you will hear, feel, resonate with, a universal throbbing. This is the heartbeat of the Cosmos, the All. Most souls eventually end up here, which is also where most begin.

With this rejoining the Oneness as the outcome, physical death, even an unconscious one, is not so miserable as it is feared to be.

STAY AWARE

There are, however, a few things to watch out for as you enter the Oneness. First, there are trick windows, pockets, soul-traps that look and feel like the Oneness, but which are not. Only the most sentient, most conscious souls can avoid these, can detect the windows that lead deceptively into a trap, and can navigate the way out should such a trap be entered. Those who enter such a trap risk perpetual enslavement by being reborn into a genetically programmed life form that uses its energy, unbeknownst to itself, in service to a cosmic hierarchy of energy domination. Stay aware to stay free. Stay aware right through all of your dyings.

If you realize that you have been enslaved as a pattern-addictable life form—an obediently self-programming entity—free yourself. Seek challenges to overcome, ways of pressuring yourself to deconstruct your programming, to reformat your energy formation. Find deaths, living deaths, through which to do this. Living death is encouraged in this instance because physical death may not offer as conscious a release from enslavement. Physical death or shedding, without proper training, training that requires dedicated study to absorb, does not provide you the marvelous opportunity to consciously master the deprogramming of the self. Deprogramming the self while tied to a physical body with its very physical neurological circuitry is a real struggle and is a marvelous challenge. This conscious deprogramming is a mastery that each and every one of us needs to practice while still living in physicality. Once this mastery is acquired, we can meet the many challenges of the nonphysical multidimensional travel we encounter when our physical bodies "die."

E I G H T SHEDDING YOUR SKIN

Each and every one of us reaches a point in life, usually several times, when our particular way of seeing the world no longer works for us. Then our particular way of behaving, of relating, of being—our particular reality—no longer fits us.

ALL DEATHS ARE A SHEDDING

We have talked about the importance of being perceptive enough to spot windows of opportunity and, even before that, of being sensitive enough to know when we are at a fork in our road. Usually, prior to coming to a fork or a window, there is a need for shedding. As with detecting forks and windows, we tend to miss seeing that we need to shed our skins until we are either deep into the process, have completed the process, or are well into a much later shedding. Or we miss our sheddings entirely, not realizing that they have taken place. This results in our not using them well or, all too frequently, our not bringing them to completion.

But shedding is as much a part of life and death as is any other function. We shed skin cells and hair every day. As adults, we have, most likely, already shed several relationships and behaviors.

People who die physical deaths shed their bodies. Basically, most of our physical deaths take place when we have outgrown or over-damaged our bodies. Our bodies are then no longer the vehicles of our spiritual evolution.

The same is true of our relationships, our jobs, our addictions, any of our behaviors. There always comes a time for shedding them. Some sheddings are complete cut-offs, endings, abrupt deaths. Other sheddings are transitions, transformations, and transcendences of the patterns *within* behaviors or relationships.

How You Know Your Skin's Too Tight

Too often the pressure to shed sneaks up on us. We finally notice that the skin of a relationship, a behavior, a life, is far too tight—that we have outgrown it the way a snake outgrows its skin.

You can get more out of the shedding process by recognizing when you are at its threshold. How do you do this? Become very alert to subtleties:

- Notice even slight shifts in your ability to concentrate.
- Notice even slight changes in your enthusiasm.
- Notice when you feel even slightly claustrophobic or trapped—physically, emotionally, intellectually, spiritually.
- Notice if you are regularly exhibiting troubled behavior (which is detrimental to yourself or others).
- Notice to what degree you function on automatic —that is, mindlessly.
- Notice how you respond when you stop for a moment's reflection and ask yourself, "Who am I and why am I here?"

If you find that your life has less and less meaning for you—pay attention. Do not assume that mere physical survival has meaning. It may, and it may not, depending on the effect upon your soul of achieving this survival. Is this struggle for physical survival building strong pattern addictions into your physicality and mentality? You are an easily controllable entity if you only succeed in surviving physically until you die physically.

You know when it is time to shed your skin. You are caged in, boxed in, trapped, by the patterns of your life; you are losing your self and your free will.

GETTING OUT

Until you see the truth, you are living a lie. Once you allow yourself to see the truth, to detect the need for shedding, you must let yourself out of your lie—out of your skin. Here's where there is, sometimes, a strong resistance. Either you or the people around you may not want you to change.

Take steps to plan the death of the body of behavior you have outgrown. Open your eyes to the forks and the windows! They are everywhere. Identify the best portals into your transformation.

Do not let anyone tell you that you cannot get there from here. This statement reveals our deep programming to believe in severe limitations. You can get anywhere you want from here. You just need a map and a vehicle.

WHY SOME PEOPLE PREFER PHYSICAL DEATH

When you are without the map and the vehicle, or have not yet found the courage to read the map and drive the vehicle, you stay quite stuck. You know the feeling: It's that phase called "paradox" described in Chapter 5. Some persons remain entirely or substantially within a paradox—the same, repeating, or similar sort of paradox—for most of their lives. When the pressure to shed becomes unbearably great, they either get sick and die or suicide and die.

While these deaths are unfortunate, traumatic, and

sad developments, they are, ironically, easy ways out when stumbled into unintentionally. Do not misunderstand this comment. Not all physical illness and terminal disease, and not all suicide, is the result of a long-term personal resistance to the shedding of paradox. A significant portion of illness and even suicide is the expression of overarching global conditions—such as the diminishing quality of food, extensive pollution, over crowding, contagion, terror—the true effects of which are too large to see for those who are untrained.

Still, some persons are trapped for a long, long time and remain resistant to dying the living death of the pattern that traps them. They see no exit, no way to shed their skins except physical death. And then, on some level, they decide to get out by becoming terminally ill or impulsively suiciding. Because the decision is usually an unconscious one, it does not seem to be a decision. Instead it is seen as an unfortunate event.

And it is indeed unfortunate, but for a very complex reason. One of the most unfortunate developments in physicality is the moving "down" of a troubled behavior pattern from the energetic to the psychological to the physical realm. This allows trapped energy to become more dense, more physical. It is not surprising that many psychological and spiritual disturbances take on a physical aspect—such as drug addiction, sex addiction, domestic violence, being accident prone, and, of course, physical pain and illness, and even suicidal tendencies. Beings who live in the material plane, as you do, pull whatever they can into a place where they can see it. This is the drive to "make real" troubled energies that are perceived but not seen.

This drive to physically manifest is valuable when it calls attention to energy disturbances and implicit pattern addictions that might not otherwise be seen. At the same time, this "physicalizing" or "somaticization" of a hidden condition can result in physical suffering without any healing or even any recognition of the condition from which it stems. Basically, you can make yourself sick pulling the energy into physical form unless you are trained to work with it.

It is best to destructure detrimental energy patterns before they become physical. This means that we must be highly conscious of these patterns long before they make themselves visible to the physical eye. Much more is accomplished when the work is done above the level of the physical body and material plane. Surgery on energy patterns is possible and essential. A forthcoming book details this treatment.

THE RIGHT TO DIE

The above is quite true. Still, even physical death can be a great teacher and releaser. This is not to advocate for the unconscious stumbling into terminal disease or impulsive or irresponsible suicide. However, this is *not* an argument against conscious physical death as a respectable way out of the skin of a life that one has outgrown. The right to die must be defended. The art and science of dying must be taught.

We already know much more about self-deliverance than we realize. Certainly, there are persons who can give advice regarding medicinal and mechanical means of dying. However, there are many ways of consciously detaching from the body that require no assistance. These essential techniques will be expressed more clearly in a later volume. You have a right to this information but only with the moral commitment to use it correctly.

HARVESTING YOUR DEATH

Once you begin to appreciate the concepts that your major transitions are all deaths and that you can master each and every one of your death processes, you begin to gain power over the course of your life and your evolution. As you grow in this understanding, you gain an increasing say in the use of your energy. Remember that you are continuously cultivating—manufacturing, generating, formatting, and transforming—your energy.

Understand your right to access energy: You can access the energy flowing through you and through any dimension of reality at any moment you choose. This is free energy. You help manufacture it. You release it, contribute it, into reality. You have as much right to energy as anyone or anything else. You have as much right to energy so long as you use it, format it, to fuel the right and honorable use of free will.

DEATH IS A GIFT

Do not fear change. Fear congests and weakens your energy. Remember that there is, throughout the Cosmos, a perpetual flow of change, in which forces are *always* interweaving and disentangling, contracting and expanding. This is called "samsura" or incessant motion by Buddhists. Some of the motion is smooth. Some of it is convulsive. Some of it is congested. But all of it is change. Change is incessant.

And so, when a change feels in any way like a death, see it as a gift. Energy is being released, changed. Change is the moving, the freeing, of energy.

Resistance to change is stagnation. A long-term paradox becomes a stagnation of energy. Too many elect, by what they believe to be their own free wills, to stagnate, to go against the flow, to resist change. This is not surprising. We have not allowed ourselves and have not been allowed to fully understand the dynamics of change. We are held in an unenlightened state because we are more easily controlled there—controlled by our own pattern addictions, our own political systems, and by other more cosmic forces too large for us to see.

The unenlightened resist change, seeing change as threatening and death as the end rather than as a shift into a new dimension of reality. The enlightened person does not resist the flow of the life force throughout the dimensions but opens to a recognition of this flow and to a movement *with* this flow. The greater our understanding of this most dynamic and divine order, the more our actions will harmonize with it.

Harmony is essential. And so is freedom. A greater, more conscious, and more vigilant understanding of the transition of energy from one dimension to another is the best defense against the kidnapping of our individual and species energy. Our energy is especially vulnerable when we are in transition. Just as there are predators in the jungle, there are forces in all dimensions which seek to use our energy arrangements and transitions and releases for their own purposes. These forces seek to subsume, trap, and enslave the energy we cultivate and release.

Preparing for the Harvest

We have touched on the notion that your energy is yours. Because you cultivate your arrangement of it and you release your arrangement of it, you are responsible for what it does and where it goes. This means that you, as a responsible being, must learn to master the flow of your energy in and out of life transitions, deaths, and dimensions of reality. You must be as conscious as possible of the phases of transition (including those described in Chapter 3), and transcendence (as described in Chapter 5). You must be ever alert for indication of sheddings, forks, and windows (as described in Chapters 6, 7, and 8). You must stay conscious through all your deaths—physical and nonphysical—in order to be certain you do not surrender, sign over, or land your energy in a place where you lose your say, lose free will, over its use without understanding the implications of this surrender.

It is your responsibility, then, to prepare for the appropriate and conscious *harvest of your energy*, which takes place during and following each and every one of your dying processes. This harvest is the reaping of your product, of the amazing force held within the configuration of self that you have constructed up to that death point.

To best prepare for your harvest, take control of your life. Although you cannot control all the events around you, you can direct and navigate your ride through them.

- Become sensitive to the phases, sheddings, forks, and windows we have discussed.
- During any difficult transition, stay focused on a high point within what you feel is your physical body, or a metaphor for a physical body. It is best to select either the area in the center of the forehead or at the top of the head to stay connected to. See a cord extending from your essence back to this area of your physical body.
- Hold on to this connection, this cord, until you understand the implications of letting go of it or

severing it. Keep returning to the idea of this cord, as if there were an actual physical cord attached, no matter what happens, no matter what shocks, waves, or dissolutions occur.

• If you decide that you really want to let go of this cord, you may, but do so quite consciously, as if you are knowingly releasing the reins while riding a wild horse. This release intensifies the transformation, the death, of your old energy matrix. Be ready for a massive release and transition. But first: Check the terrain out. Are there any traps or trick windows leading to dead ends or undesirable nests for your energy? These must be avoided. Can you see clearly what is calling you and coming at you? Another volume in this series will detail the various releases of the cord that you might undertake at this juncture. For now, letting go, yet being highly conscious as you do, is enough of a description.

• Should you elect this form of profound release, intense severance, do so knowing that, unless you are trained in preserving your individual essence, you are freeing your energy for absorption by your environment in time, in space, in the Cosmos. The harvest of your energy will no longer be specifically yours then.

• To turn over your harvest, the release of energy brought about by your dying process, is not a detrimental choice, so long as you know well where you are sending it. No matter how rough your ride, how tortured your dying process, it is your responsibility to keep your eyes—your sensory mechanisms—open and to notice what systems are there to receive your energy. This is one of the greatest and most exciting challenges faced by life forms throughout the Cosmos.

• Whether you are dying the death of a behavior or dying a physical death, you must take responsibility for the energy you release when old patterns die. The harvest is yours. Stay conscious of this. Do not sell your product, the arrangement of energy you have cultivated, at the market unless the exchange is toward an ever more right use and freedom of will. If you feel unprepared to make such an assessment, keep your energy under your wing and continue to evolve it.

TEN

FROM PERSONAL APOCALYPSE INTO POWER

Life is not necessarily easy, but it is a tremendous experience. Many say that it is better to have lived than never to have lived at all. What do you think? As a human in a physical body, you certainly know the ordeals faced by life forms living in the third dimension. These ordeals can encourage your spiritual growth. They can also distract you from spiritual growth. The journey through your human incarnation is superbly challenging. And the potential for what is called "the quickening of the soul" is profoundly immense during your human incarnation. Try to remember this in your living moments of mortal anguish. And try to receive this message in its entirety at the hour of your physical death.

The Denial of More
Beyond the Physical

As physical humans, it is very easy for us to think that nothing exists but this third dimension—that there is only material reality and nothing else—and therefore, that all life forms and celestial forms have physical bodies. Although we often begin to feel that there might be more to our reality than meets the physical eye, and even that there is a God, the popularly operating assumption remains that nothing living can really exist without a three-dimensional body.

As our spiritual awareness matures or evolves, there is a developing of higher, less physical domains of the self. As we extend our awareness of reality beyond the base physical realm, we become less and less physical, less and less dense, and more and more aware of our expansion into realms less physically dense than a physical body. Try to encourage this trend in yourself. You will be contributing to your own and your species' evolution.

The essence of the universe lies beyond the grasp of the existing human intellect manifesting in physicality. Fortunately, the collective human mind is beginning to progress through the development of its intellect into a new form of intelligence. The new intelligence, with its new form of rationality, pragmatically confirms rather than cognitively denies more beyond the physical.

THE IMPORTANCE OF DENSITY

A deeper respect for density is essential here, both to ease the passage from physical death to the beyond, and, while in this particular lifetime of yours, to understand how programming and pattern addictions can be transcended. In reading the following review, remember that it helps to think in pictures in order to make an understanding of density work for you. You are, in a sense, being asked to "lighten up," to de-densify. In a less dense form, your energy is lighter, more malleable, more easily rearranged. Physical programming can be altered or suspended when it is ascended into a less dense state.

Light is a great teacher of density. Use your ideas about light to learn density. Attempt to see the light described below as a gleaming river of energy.

- Imagine that you are turning into light. The less dense, the more like fluid light, that you allow yourself to become, the greater your awareness will grow.
- Fluid light has almost no density. Beings, life forms, take on varying degrees of density. A life form locates along a continuum of most dense to least dense. You can move along this continuum: As you turn to light, in its many forms, you move up into less dense realms.
- Within each dimension the least dense life forms are the most evolved. As you grow in conscious-

ness, your awareness, your mentality, becomes less dense and thus more expanded. This can feel "ungrounding" to those unschooled in this process, because gravity has a lesser pull on you.

- By your inching your awareness up the scale of decreasing density, your mind and your soul become less weighed down by the compactness of belief in physical reality as the only reality. As this "unweighting" takes place, the actual *diminishing of your body relative to the expansion of your energy* begins. You may feel crazed by this sensation, as if you are "losing it," becoming "unglued." If so, relax. You are experiencing the marvelously unsettling effects of decohesion, or diminishing cohesion. You are really feeling the effect of enhanced entropy, which is the tendency of a physical system to spin out, dissolve, disintegrate, wear down, die. This is all right.

- Understand that as the physical matter, the energy, of "you" becomes less tightly organized, less rigidly formatted in a material sense, it has the opportunity to become more complex in a multidimensional sense. As matter becomes less physical, less dense, less compact, less cohesive, it dissipates increasingly. It weighs less and less per square millimeter and is thus less weighed down.

Try not to think about this too much. Misunderstanding reality is one of the dangers of over-intellectualizing important concepts. Just allow these ideas to be with you. After a while the ideas will be comprehensible.

Your mastery of death transitions requires your ability to shift densities, first in your imagination and then in your essence. You can learn this. Just remember that the most dense life forms are found in the lower dimensions where essences are most compact. The least dense life forms are found in the higher dimensions of reality. Understand that compactness and density accompany each other. Practice shrinking and expanding yourself in your mind's eye, moving toward a growing sense of becoming an increasingly luminous, beautiful form of pure light as you expand.

Third-dimensional beings and objects such as humans are not the most dense. Those found in the denser dimensions, the zero, first, and second, are far more dense and compact. Still, human incarnates are indeed quite dense, as are all physical bodies.

CONSCIOUSNESS TECHNOLOGY

Awaken your consciousness. As stated above, learning to move your being through densities is essential. To do so, you must become increasingly adept in the *consciousness technology*, of which this book and subsequent volumes on death technology are part. Consciousness technology is the method by which consciousness can become highly aware of itself and profoundly enhance its functioning and freedom. This awareness is also called "metacognition," which is a beyond-normal-thinking form of mind work.

You are definitely able to manifest your essence in increasing complexity and vastness throughout all the dimensions. You, just as any life form, can evolve increasing degrees of consciousness. You are already part of a life system of conscious interaction—a social system that has a government and an economy. But how much freedom is available to you within the system you "belong to?" And where is your rightful seat in the cosmic hierarchy? A higher level of consciousness must be achieved in order to answer these questions and to preserve free will.

REACHING THROUGH TO THE SUPERMIND

To find truth and freedom, you must learn to recognize the true, highest, purest, most light, most conscious, "supermind." Untrained, your efforts may not reach you through to the supermind or may carry you to a force that appears to be the supermind but is not. Your ignorance may not manage to transcend itself or protect you. So how do you, with physical reality limitations, ascend to your rightful place in the cosmic hierarchy of energy?

Your ascendance can be actuated by the "consciousness force," which works toward the emergence of its powers in each being's—in this case *your*—consciousness. You can allow this "superconscience" to descend into you and uplift you, to bring the process of *your* transcendence and ascendance back to your rightful level of high consciousness. *However, you must wait until you have studied subtle realities enough to know when you are in contact with the true superconscience and not a force posing as the superconscience.* Otherwise, you are surrendering your energy to a higher power, but not necessarily the higher power you would choose of your own free will had you enough information to do so. This concept is important here, in that during the dying process, whether it is a living transition or a physical shedding, energy is released. As noted elsewhere in this book, this energy is sometimes released to other than a person's own consciousness. For example, in the instance of a common living death, many persons recovering from explicit addictions are overwhelmed by their newly released energy and quickly give it away again. Sometimes they trap it in the same or a new pattern addiction. Sometimes they surrender the energy to a higher power; and only sometimes is this the true oneness of the true supermind. Too many transfer their addictions to the lure of false light. How sad it is that we have been so uniformed about our death transitions as to allow this to happen.

You *can* evolve without outside intervention, even without higher power assistance. The elements of the higher consciousness you seek are already present within *you.* Accessing these and developing these is the challenge. Decide for yourself whether to rise to this challenge. But decide consciously and stay conscious. The journe*y is yours. Travel it your way.*

BELIEVING IN MORE AND FINDING THE TRUTH ABOUT IT

Most life forms see so little of what is really here. Life forms define their realities based upon the illusions they allow themselves to believe in. All they really see are shadows of truth, shadows of reality. In these shadows live the illusions that hold us captive.

Turn on the light! Death is not what you may believe it to be! Nothing dies in the so-called "conventional" sense because nothing stops moving—matter, whether organic or inorganic, is always in motion.

Examine information for truth. Humans must do this. Truth has been severely distorted by language and culture. The precious consciousness of humanity is buried within an elaborate hierarchy of distortion that veils truth. *Human words and beliefs are part of this elaborate distortion.* A spiritual truth, to be honestly relayed in its wholeness, cannot be distorted. A spiritual truth, without ever being intellectualized by the brain of a human or any other life form, can congeal into an experience, an awareness, an image, or a symbol. That experience, awareness, image or symbol can again unfold in the eye of its beholder, depending upon the sophistication and readiness of the beholder, into varying degrees of truth.

Let this unfolding begin within you. When you are ready to understand the truth, you will recognize it as it comes to you. You only take on the degree of truth you are ready to handle.

POWER IS IN KNOWING WHO YOU ARE

Know who you are. Know that every individual soul is a microconsciousness, one that affects the macroconsciousness. Every soul vibrates at its own frequency of consciousness and this frequency can be raised, evolved by that soul. Spiritual evolution is a constant developing of form, of spiritual form. Development involves journeying through all dimensions of reality. The sole purpose of any spirit's coming into the third dimension of reality (such as on the physical Earth) is to work toward manifesting what is called the "indwelling spirit."

When free to, physical nature evolves in this direction; the progression is from physicality or matter toward higher mind or nonphysicality. The evolution of matter through time is from the lower to the higher dimensions. Every soul has the right to ascend to a higher consciousness.

You are a great soul. You can bring the energy generated by a transformation of your own consciousness to the collective energy pool. You can contribute to a global, a cosmic, transformation that will help end the dictatorial cultivation, wasting, and kidnapping of your physical-plane and ethereal energies.

Commit to this growth for the good of us all. Your great soul has the potential to advance the evolution of humanity, of other souls whether human or not, and to spread true enlightenment.

Always seek authenticity in the expression of your power—do not be fooled by the temptations of self-doubt and negativity. If you are nonchalant and noncommittal, you are surrendering to enslavement, to greater pattern addiction, to the capturing and killing of free will! *You can help to protect free will by becoming free.*

Now that we have said that there is no such thing as death, an elaboration on this is necessary. There is a great difference between cyclical death and absolute death. When free will disappears entirely from the Cosmos, this will be the absolute death of free will. Matter and energy may live on eternally; however, the will can be permanently eliminated. This tragic elimination is not an adventure in death. This is the end of the life of an energy force we have come to call "freedom." Do not allow this transition into an entirely mechanical, programmed, robotic, will-less, soul-less universe to happen. Do not become a robot. Do not populate the machine race with the precious essence you have cultivated. Do not let your energy become fuel in an evolutionary progression you do not support. Stay highly conscious. Make all your deaths a contribution to the positive evolution of will.

ELEVEN — REVOLUTION AND DEATH

They say we think, therefore we are. But who are we? What thinks? The brain? The mind? Is there a difference? And what is this behavior we call thinking?

Contained in a skull no larger than a deflated soccer ball and physically manifested in the form of a wrinkled blob we call *brain,* the human mind is a cagey, intractable entity—difficult to locate but boundaryless, capable of amazing feats but weak and fallible, seemingly autonomous and yet tending toward the convenience of supposedly "survival-oriented preprogramming" that often results in undesirable, sometimes terrible, habitual behaviors and other pattern addictions.

One of the toughest of all our pattern addictions is the addiction to our reality. Somehow, we allow our dependence on what is known, our deep reliance on our reality, to be a reality check on *all* reality. We cling to "what is," refusing to let it die unless we are pushed to the edge and lose control or fitfully relinquish it. And then there is a tortured death rather than a fruitful one.

When the world as we know it, the reality upon which we have become so dependent, dies, do we die too? Must we die too?

They say that we live, therefore we die. But who says this? Who lives? What dies?

Could we be prisoners of a lie?

THE POLITICS OF DEATH

Could death be something different than what we have come to believe? Can we break free of the shackles of our realities and see through our fears, our sufferings, our difficult transitions, our mental, emotional, spiritual, and even physical deaths? Can we look through the veil of deception that humanity has allowed itself to live beneath *and see truth*?

YES! But first we must be willing enough, be daring enough, to ask:

Are we programmed to die? Why do each and every one of our cells have a genetic plan to die off after a certain number of divisions?

Are we genetically programmed to die physical deaths? Or are we genetically programmed to believe that we have to die and that death is final? And is this programmed-in belief so all-powerful that it controls us, kills us, commandeers our wills, and makes our deaths final?

We have been brainwashed into acceptance of the lie about dying. What for? What force or intelligence or energy could have focused upon our genetic coding so closely to create such a limited reality in our minds?

We must dare to ask: Are we biological, fleshy robots? Do we reflect a shallow mechanical light in our eyes, the light of will-lessness, the glow of hypnotization? Have we succumbed to a mandated daze in modern years or have we always been part of a very large mindlessness—are we biotech at its finest? Or biotech gone wrong?

If Earth is a fantastic macrocosmic laboratory and we are prisoner-subjects in a massive experiment too large for our human minds to fathom, then our learning the truth can lead to startling discoveries regarding our captors. Perhaps we can capture control of our wills and set them free.

Only a revolution of human awareness can free us. But what would this freedom look like? Would it be much different than the way we live and look now? Can we really be free as long as we are subject to the enslavement of inherited and acquired, genetic and neurological, programming? Can we find freedom while living in the material plane?

BREAKING THROUGH THE SHACKLES
OF OUR PROGRAMMING

These questions are more readily asked than answered. Yet we might move toward an inkling of an answer if we reflect upon the degrees of freedom allowed us by biology. Consider that, as physical beings, we function on genetic and neurological automatic the majority of the time, yet we fool ourselves into believing that we exercise a great deal of free will. We are in a state of denial about our mechanical, robotic, programmed, and programmable nature.

We living things are creatures of habit. As was explained in the previous chapters, our ability to biologically (and even genetically) program ourselves for automatic responses is essential for survival. Speedy responses to danger, for example, save lives. If we had to take time to think through each action, we would probably die off. We rely on our automatic behaviors to respond to physical events such as falling objects and red traffic lights and other situations that demand a quick response. We also may respond automatically to seemingly less critical physical events or conditions such as hunger for a snack, a cold draft in the house, or a baby's cry. Some pieces of this behavior are genetically inherited and thus instinct driven; and other pieces are the result of patterning acquired during day-to-day experiences.

So convenient and readily developed is automatic

physical behavior that it merges with the nonphysical realms of human interaction and emotion. Public and private feelings, and their expressions, are often manifestations of psychological and social patterns. It is difficult to discern exactly what proportion of an individual's behavior is attributable to the larger social and cultural environment, and what proportion is particular, idiosyncratic to the individual.

It is also difficult to separate the larger social and political behaviors of the human population on Earth from the genetic programming nested within each cell of every human.

Previous chapters have suggested that this ambiguity is especially true in blatant cases of drug addiction. Add to this explicit addiction our general addictions to sweets and our over consumption of food whenever we can pay for it. So much of our cultural overlay is dedicated to the selling and feeding of food and at least legal drugs to the consumer—the consumer who is starving for truth, love, and freedom. We are bombarded by advertisements to eat food, drink alcohol, and take painkillers. Is overconsumption, or addiction to these things, merely an individual malady, or is it an acquired response to environmental stimulation? Even if this question could be definitively answered, there is still the matter of programming. Once a behavior, no matter what its origin, is repeated a number of times, a program is written into the neural pathways that have transmitted the biochemical message required to repeat the act. The more repetition, the deeper the programming, the more automatic the behavior. The robot within us rises, run by automatic programming, at once the prison and the prisoner of gene-based physical life. Meet the biological robot: you, me, everyone.

DEATH AS ERASURE OF PROGRAMMING

There is no way, except perhaps physical death, to clear the brain of all past impressions and programming. Those who believe in the spillover of experience from lifetime to lifetime will claim that even physical death is not a guaranteed clearing of the mind. But let us say, for argument's sake, that physical, biological, death is an effective means of erasure, and that only this sort of death offers complete erasure. Biological death, then, is a sure means of overcoming or transcending a problematic personal condition, especially if the problem condition is, as are most conditions of human behavior, subject to neurological and other forms of biological patterning. Physical death, under appropriate circumstances, is an honorable option.

Or maybe physical death is not a complete erasure but, instead, a sort of amnesia, allowing whatever it is that may live on when the body dies a chance to forget its biological programming. What a marvelous opportunity this might be for those who are deeply dissatisfied with the programming that they have either inherited or acquired. We cannot, however, be certain that all deaths guarantee even some degree of suspension or transcendence of programming. It is therefore as important to die well, consciously, as it is to live well, consciously. Conscious preparation for death is preparation for conscious transcendence.

Again, this is not an advocacy of conscious physical death as the only way out of problem conditions. Too many lives turn around, too many healings and recoveries take place, to believe that there is no way except physical death to escape unpleasant patterns. Physical death is merely one category of death along a continuum, or a matrix, of deaths.

Death, whatever form it may take, offers the opportunity for transcendence but in no way guarantees it. Again, it is important to die well, whether or not the death in question is biological. A death can be life healing and therefore purifying when conducted with focus and awareness.

BECOMING A SPIRITUAL REVOLUTIONARY

Programmed people are not free; they are robots proceeding to function as programmed. Whatever bit of the soul nestles within the heart of a pattern-addicted being is trapped, caged, suffocating. Too many spirits allow themselves to be suffocated by patternings, eventually permanently extinguishing themselves. Any Master Plan or Blueprint, if you believe there is one, that would have planned for this development, must be overthrown. Too many souls are being enslaved, turned into robots, lost. The massive stagnating and extinguishing of the free will of human souls threatens the perpetuation of freedom within all Creation.

You become a sort of revolutionary when you master death. This is because the limits to your reality, your prison walls, will be broken through by you in the process of transcendence. Why not reap the benefits of your own death, of the tremendous purification you can bring about if you transcend your fear and stay conscious?

The process of breaking addiction to a destructive pattern is a revolutionary experience for an individual. It also has revolutionary implications for society, because transcending addiction calls for fundamental changes in the way that a pattern-addicted person sees the world. For an addicted world to transcend pattern addiction, all of the human race must see all of reality with new eyes.

When people change their world views, they inevitably affect the lives of the people around them. Through this process, every time any sort of addiction is transcended, there are political ramifications. Imagine all of us breaking our addiction to this reality at the same time!

THE POLITICS OF HEALING

So, as hundreds of thousands of citizens are treated for explicit pattern addictions such as chemical dependence and overeating, and for physical diseases caused by deep energy pattern addictions, the people and organizations that treat these addicted individuals are wielding extraordinary political power—affecting the world view of their clients and patients. Treatment professionals and healers are in a position to encourage a large number of individuals to undergo *radical* changes in their behavior and mind-sets. When these "healed" individuals reenter society, they can go on to affect their friends, relatives, and coworkers. They can vote for elected officials and buy consumer goods. They can raise healthy children and form a large part of the future. Indeed, recovering, *discovering*, addicts can become a powerful political force if they are mobilized. And if we expand the group of addicted persons as far as we can, to include those suffering from all kinds of other pattern-based psychological and physical illusions and afflictions, once they are healed, we have a massive army of persons who can march ahead of society, leading the way down the path of transcendence. What a liberation army these "healed" people could be!

Is their political potential at the mercy of the treatment community? Can their doctors ever really be their teachers? Well, yes and no. There are many, many caring and concerned members of the health care community who are actively seeking to aid their clients and patients in the struggle to transcend addictions and afflictions. But the sad truth is that much of the health care community has become mired in the "traditional" concept of the addicted and afflicted person's path and plight. As a result, the health establishment has become complacent and comfortable in its naive beliefs that:

- Pattern addictions must be explicit to be read.
- Only members of the health care establishment can detect and diagnose a health problem.
- The diagnosis that the health care establishment makes is the only diagnosis possible and the only diagnosis that is correct.
- Observed symptoms have only certain, predetermined, official diagnoses.
- The treatment of the symptom called for by a diagnosis is the only correct treatment.
- All symptoms are exactly what they appear to be.
- If the health care establishment does not see the underlying implicit pattern addiction, the underlying implicit pattern addiction is not there.
- When what appears to be the same symptom turns up in two different individuals, both individuals are treatable in the same way.
- Alternative forms of treatment are unnecessary.
- Only those exhibiting the symptoms need treatment.

- The officially designated treatment will work.
- The original symptoms will be eased or will disappear when the malady is ameliorated or eliminated.
- If things get better, the prescribed *treatment* is working; if things stay the same or get worse, the *patient* is not working, i.e., not properly following the prescribed treatment.

But these claims are not true. Think about it. A lot of doctors and hospitals and insurance companies have a financial stake in maintaining old, well-established perceptions. Economic bodies such as corporations and governments buy health insurance and managed care services in bulk for their employees and constituents. Insurance companies pay for traditional forms of treatment because that is the type of coverage that companies and governments will buy; companies and governments buy this coverage because that is what the insurance companies and public third party payers will pay for. Vast profits would be lost if the diagnosis and subsequent treatment of chemical dependence or other health afflictions such as cancer changed radically. By controlling the diagnostic and treatment processes, the health establishment has a stranglehold on the way we think about addiction and all illnesses. Healing has become secondary to maintaining a profit margin. Old ideas die hard, especially when loss of dollars is involved. Instead of seeking radical transformation in the definition and diagnosis of mental and physical afflictions, including chemical dependence, the health establishment perpetuates its diagnostic monopoly. The work of transcending pattern addiction, truly obliterating the programming that causes disease, remains on the back burner.

And so we continue to suffer from an information breakdown. Information regarding the true nature and health consequences of pattern addiction does not circulate because it cannot circulate easily. How could the establishment adopt a revised diagnosis of pattern addiction for most illnesses? How would the process of death described in this book be prescribed to heal patterning?

For example, in recent decades, it has become painfully obvious that drug addiction is not the problem the health establishment has defined it as being. Diagnosis has a political component. We should be diagnosing the entire global society, not separate individuals. Until we are willing to face this global diagnosis, we are at war with truth. We are experiencing massive societal denial about chemical dependence and many other explicit addictions including those to sex, spending, relationships, food, violence, and television. We are experiencing massive societal—species—denial about all underlying pattern addictions in the same way that individuals deny their addictions. The entire species is addicted to its implicit patterns. No one living in a physical body is exempt. (Those who have left their bodies are not necessarily out of range of such programming either.)

FREE WILL AND
THE PATTERN-ADDICTED SOCIETY

Let's continue our focus on chemical dependence for the moment because it is easier to understand the ramifications of an explicit addiction than it is to see the pervasive presence of implicit pattern addiction. Could it be that in some subtle way our global society is working to keep large numbers of its members dependent on chemicals, or similarly addicted to other detrimental patterns? Again, we must ask: Are we biotechnology at its finest, or biotechnology gone wrong? And, do we really have a say in this condition?

Think about the implications of your own addictions. A little addict person—an implant—has been placed deep inside you. He lurks deep down in your subconscious, waiting for an opportunity to "drive" you—to commandeer your decision-making processes. You may think that you live free, but you are deluding yourself. You are actually a prisoner of your little addict implant-person, and he will eventually find and exploit your weaknesses and your resistance to death—if he hasn't done so already. How readily we succumb to the subtle but continuous diminishing of human freedom when we obediently trade away personal freedom for pattern addiction. Free will slips away.

To relinquish the freedom of responsibility, of self-control, to an automatic addiction is, in modern lingo, a cop-out. Rather than cope with reality, you let your little addict person feed you mechanisms that muffle your consciousness, stifle the stresses of life along with your alertness, offer you illusions of relief—vacations from demands. These mechanisms come in the form of obsessions with foods, sex, relationships, shopping, gambling, or other things or behaviors.

Eventually, the wonderful and usually subconscious lie of pattern addiction turns sour—but by then it is too late. You have become a slave to your patterning. Only an internal revolution of phenomenal proportions can set you free again. Transcendence is this revolution.

Understanding what it means to say, "I am addicted to my patterns," is a difficult process. Feeling what it takes to know, "I am an addict," is painful. Acknowledging that you are an addicted individual precipitates a sense of *ought to*—a pressure to break the cycle of pattern addiction, to let some part of the self die. That *ought to* begins to lurk in the innermost recesses of the self, where the free will and the living soul have retreated.

We all must hear this: The anguish of exorcising an invader, of ripping out an automatic pattern or implant that has taken you over, that you have embedded within your own nervous system, makes it easier to stay with the addiction than to cut it out of your life. Breaking the unwieldy, intractable habit cycle seems as impossible as turning the tide or halting an avalanche. The myopic and eventually blind security of pattern addiction seems relatively comfortable when you are staring into the face of harsh reality—personal responsibility and freedom. For the pattern-addicted individual there is always the fear that reality will hurt more than addiction. Mindless obedience often appears more comfortable than profound change, and slavery safer than freedom.

Surrender to any damaging pattern addiction is a countersoul experience. Addiction with no release from it eventually causes an individual to undergo soul death—a false, aspiritual, and yet tragic death in which the loss of self becomes final, succumbing to an absolute unwillingness to let detrimental programming die. Progressive addictive behavior is a process of surrender in which the *will is eroded* until the will of the individual eventually disappears. A healthy, conscious death of any sort, as is encouraged in this book, becomes nearly impossible. Independent decision-making capabilities are commandeered by robotic, mechanical tendencies. The human biotechnology rolls over and plays machine, soul dead.

As free will and self-control erode away, *a vacuum of vulnerability* is left inside the mind of the pattern-addicted individual. This vacuum sucks in outside agents: viruses, foreign energy patterns, chemicals, detrimental forms of relationships to other people, obsessions with sex, associations with unhealthy connections, adherence to the dictums of cult leaders. Opportunistic physical diseases, social forces, organizations, and intelligences move in and take control. They take over the decision-making processes that could have been controlled by the free will of the individual. When this happens, we surrender our basic human rights to *individual power,* to the realization of our own spirituality, and therefore to the power and spirit of our collective humanity.

The truth about the advance of pattern addiction is that it has prepared us to be ever more unwittingly controlled—to not only relinquish our free will, but worse, *to forget what free will is.* This is the most insidious politic of pattern addiction. We are denying our own freedom when we fail to acknowledge the larger picture. Blind denial is a losing stance. *It is time to become conscious and to pay attention.* It is time to actively ferret out *and let die* our most damaging implicit as well as explicit pattern addictions. Let our prison walls fall as our addictions to this reality die; it is time for us to break free and transcend. The lie must die.

Indeed, we are at a critical juncture in time—in the history of life and time. What you do on Earth while embodied in physical reality (the third dimension) is going to make a great difference. You can contribute to a great and most necessary rebalancing. You can support the fight for free will by beginning with your own liberation, by letting the prisoner within you die. Take back your right to consciously die all your own deaths.

FREEING THE DYING HEART

Highly sensitive, feeling people are an endangered species. Their hearts are hiding, dying. Their lives are wounded by the brainwashing they carry regarding death. They are being forced into chemicalization, narcotization, mechanization, and robotization. They retreat from a high degree of sensitivity to the stress, hassle, and pain of modern life to save themselves from death. But then, they risk killing off their souls. Without contact, without inspiration, life can be very difficult. Some of us break down. Some of us get sick. Some of us die unconscious deaths. And some just live in the limbo of soul death, the most false, unhealthy, and absolute death of all.

Anyone addicted to his or her reality and definition of reality is dangerously pattern-addicted. This is just about everyone. Pattern-addicted individuals have made both little and big decisions, over a period of time, to trade away free will, the freedom of self-control, in order to avoid and to numb the challenges and pains of living. In so doing, addicted people have selected the path without the heart. They have decided to live like machines—or practically like machines, many with false feelings and pseudo-loves dressed to appear real. They have become creatures of habit—increasingly mechanical women and men. The life within their souls is draining away. "And a rock feels no pain." Nor does a machine.

Ultimately, it is death, death and the purest of love, that can free the addicted, programmed, person in all of us and turn humanity away from the path of the robot. Seek the highest path for your human heart. Love can transcend the intense lure of the land of no feeling—the seemingly safe but very empty place of the dead heart. We can raise the matrix of love out of this third dimension to heal it. Through this ascension of love comes the resurrection of free will.

Something strange is happening to love. It is slipping away from us—all of us. Or perhaps we never quite understood love. Deciding to find high order love and to feel such love is the first step in freeing humanity's dying heart, in life healing. In this effort, we must all become like children taking our first steps, learning to explore the precious and fragile land of our truest feelings. In so doing, we preserve what is most human about us in an environment that pressures us to be more distant from our hearts, more machinelike, more automatic, every day. You can help transcend the pressure to surrender free will and the will to love. You can transcend. Yes, you can effectively harvest each and every one of the deaths you undergo.

Do not be afraid to die. See yourself as an emissary of truth. Take your heightened awareness and purified love into all that lies beyond the walls of the material dimension. Consciously harvest the transcendence your death brings! Transcendence is life healing. Transcendence is freedom. Transcendence is your ascension into new realms. And high love will fuel your, our, ascension.

When you fully embrace death, you will know. You will set the captive free. You will fly through the portal of change into new worlds. You will rise from the ashes of challenge, transition, enslavement, and even seeming disaster, in splendor: the Phoenix transcending.

THE PORTAL

Acknowledgments

I wish to thank the many souls I have met on the path to life. I name but a few here. My biological father and biological mother, both of whom shared with me, in great detail, with stark intimacy, with naked hearts, their journeys into the enormous transition we call physical death, one of whom invited me to initiate his process for him—the literal initiation which I declined—both of whom contacted me and continued teaching me from the beyond. My unearthly spiritual guide, Dr. Leo Zeff, who could not be on the planet for the writing of this book, pointed me down the path of transcendence, and allowed me the honor of teaching him what he already knew so very well, and showed me his death transition. My honorable and megamind teacher, Gregory Bateson, who has also left the planet, taught me the importance of the double bind in promoting transcendence and in all higher level learning. And I thank my dear friend and distant cousin, the poet Victor diSuvero, who, by happenstance and synchronicity, has found me, and sings to me the connection between peace and despair with his bridge of visionary imagery. And I must thank Robert Stricker, Robert Shubow, and Shirley Smith for their assistance, love, and wisdom. And I thank expert word processing and layout whiz, Leona Jamison, for saving me time and again, above and beyond the call of duty. Most of all, I thank the brave keepers of the light who continue to light the way. You know who you are. You brave a path of free will—and hope and love and light—through the imprisoned dimension that is ever more ruled by the ever more dominant counterspirit. You point the way to freedom—the way to spiritual survival. I met you along the way and I know I will see you there.

131

About the Author

Angela Browne-Miller, also known as *shri-yah*, is a spiritual scientist, psychotherapist, author, musician, painter, and mother. She holds two masters degrees (one in public health and one in social welfare) and two doctorates (one in social welfare and one in education) from the University of California, Berkeley. Dr. Browne-Miller's areas of research and publication include ancient and modern metaphysics, social policy and political science, education and intelligence, mental health, health care, addiction, child development, and the special problems of modern women. Her many books, articles, illustrations, and photographs have appeared extensively, both nationally and internationally, in lay and professional presses such as the *International Journal of Law and Psychiatry*, the *International Child Welfare Review*, the *San Francisco Chronicle*, and *Family Circle*. She has discussed her work on national and local television and radio programs such as *Talk of the Nation*, the *Oprah Winfrey Show*, and major network documentaries, and at conferences and institutes including the National Broadcasters Association, The Aspen Institute, Esalen, the Whole Life Expo, the U.S. Army War College, and the American Academy of Psychotherapists. She has served as a policy analyst for the White House Conference on Families, on the U.S. Office of Juvenile Justice Task Force on Drug Abuse, as a lecturer at the University of California, Berkeley, and as a post-doctor fellow at the National Institute of Mental Health. Dr. Browne-Miller has worked with several thousand people in psychotherapeutic contexts, addressing lifestyle change, pattern-addiction relief, spiritual transformation, and the death release.